Optimist
HANDBOOK

By
Alan Williams

© RYA Optimist Handbook
© Alan Williams 2009
First Published 2009

The Royal Yachting Association
RYA House, Ensign Way
Hamble, Southampton
Hampshire SO31 4YA

Tel: 0845 345 0400
Fax: 0845 345 0329
E-mail: publications@rya.org.uk
Web: www.rya.org.uk

ISBN 978-1-905104-680
RYA Order Code G44

Note: While all reasonable care had been taken in the preparation of this book, the publisher takes no responsibility for the use of the methods or products or contracts described in the book.

Telephone 0845 345 0400 for a free copy of our Publications Catalogue.

Acknowledgements

I would like to thank everybody who has helped me write this book. My main inspiration comes from the sailors I work with and the smile on their faces when they put into practice the new skills they have learned.

Duncan Truswell, the RYA Junior Racing Manager and Alan Olive, former RYA Coaching Manager have been a great inspiration and thanks to David Campbell-James for all of his help and advice and Phil Williams-Ellis from the RYA for her help and guidance in publishing this book.

I have worked closely with Welsh Yachting Association for many years particularly Tim Hall, and previously Isy Hutchinson who have always been very supportive.

Thanks also to the Sports Council for Wales whose National Watersports Centre Plas Menai I have had the privilege of managing for the past 14 years and where I have had many happy years messing about in boats.

The coaches I work with continue to inspire me including Brian Staite, Kirsty Bonar, Ollie Green and Chris Gowers the Head Olympic Sailing Coach who is also the technical editor of this book.

Thanks to Dr Frank Newton for medical advice on hiking technique.

The sailors who feature in this book are representative of the many sailors I have worked with so if you don't feature – my apologies.

Finally and most importantly thanks to Jennifer my wife for all her support and for all the days I am away coaching!

Totally Chlorine Free · Sustainable Forests · EMAS VERIFIED ENVIRONMENTAL MANAGEMENT

Published by **The Royal Yachting Association**
RYA House, Ensign Way, Hamble, Southampton
SO31 4YA

Tel: 0845 345 0400
Fax: 0845 345 0329
Email: publications@rya.org.uk
Web: www.rya.org.uk

© 2009 Alan Williams

Note: While all reasonable care has been taken in the preparation of this book, the publisher takes no responsibility for the use of the methods or products or contracts described in the book.

Cover design: Pete Galvin
Typeset: Batt Creative
Illustrations: Richard Lloyd
Illustrations page 248, 251: Claudia Myatt
Proof-reading and indexing: Alan Thatcher
Printed by: Printed in China through World Print

CONTENTS

I first met Alan many years ago when I went for selection onto the Welsh Optimist Squad at Plas Menai in North Wales. It was a bit windy so I didn't sail that much but I did enough to get into the squad.

Every winter Alan coached us and during the summers we went to lots of events. Eventually on home waters in Pwllheli in the summer of 2002 I managed to win the National Championships and I know that as I crossed the line Alan had a tear in his eye, all the hard work had paid off. It was the first time a girl had won the Nationals. Claire Lasko was the Junior National Champion the same year.

In 2003 Alan was our coach at the World Championships in Gran Canaria and after a poor start I finished 5th overall and the Girls' World Champion. That was our most successful year ever with Richard Mason 10th, and Greg Carey who led the Worlds for a few days 12th.

Optimist sailing provides all the basic skills needed to make progress from junior to youth and even Olympic level sailing and as I crossed the line after winning the Women's 420 Worlds in Gran Canaria in 2006 I remembered Alan's words 'just do it'.

This book will give you lots of hints, tips and ideas to help you know what you need to do to develop your sailing, I hope you enjoy it.

I have had some great coaching to help me progress and I think that the most important thing is to make sure you know what you need to do and then practise until you can do it.

Optimist sailing is great fun, you can learn loads and make lots of new friends as well. Thanks Alan…

Hannah Mills

Optimist Girls' World Champion
Women's 420 World Champion.

Welcome to the RYA Optimist Handbook. The aim of this book is to help you to understand the basics, develop your skills and provide you with top tips and handy hints that could help you win a championship. Be warned though, Optimist sailing is totally addictive, for sailors, parents and coaches. Sailing is a lifelong sport and from those first few tentative moments afloat, expect to spend the rest of your life messing about in boats.

The Optimist is one of the best known sailboats in the world and is great as an introduction for youngsters to the world of sailing. We are grateful to the American boat designer Clark Mills who made it all possible. In 1947 he designed the Optimist which was built from sheets of plywood and parts available at a hardware store. The boat is 2.31 metres (7 feet 6 inches) long, 1.13 metres (3 feet 8 inches) wide and weighs in at 35kg (77lbs). There are over 150,000 registered worldwide but many more have been built and the Optimist is sailed in more than 110 countries.

The original boats were made of plywood, then glass fibre boats were produced and finally from 1995 all Optimists were standardised with the 'IODA 95' hull (International Optimist Dinghy Association). This now means that all Optimists are virtually identical (one-design) and it is the sailor's skill which wins a race.

In 1965 The International Optimist Dinghy Association [IODA] came into being and in 1966 the first world championships were held in the USA.

Today the Optimist is sailed as a basic training boat each year introducing many youngsters to our sport and is also competed in at local clubs, nationally and worldwide by many young sailors who go on in various classes to represent their countries in later years at the Olympic Games.

The first part of this book covers the basics and goes on to cover more advanced techniques so, if you are already an experienced Optimist sailor, you can skip the basic boat handling section.

Often there are no absolutely right answers in sailing and while this book provides you with many ideas, hopefully, you will develop many more of your own.

Have fun!

Alan Williams
Caernarfon 2008

Make sure your boat is set up correctly

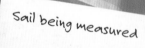

Sail being measured

Kit for Sailing

'Boat set up and tuning
is really important if
you want a fast boat'

David Evans
2nd Optimist European Championships
29er World Champion
49er sailor

Setting up the Boat
The Rig
Clothing

We'll start off looking at how to set up your boat, you might not yet be a world class sailor, but there's nothing to stop your boat being just as good as the rest.

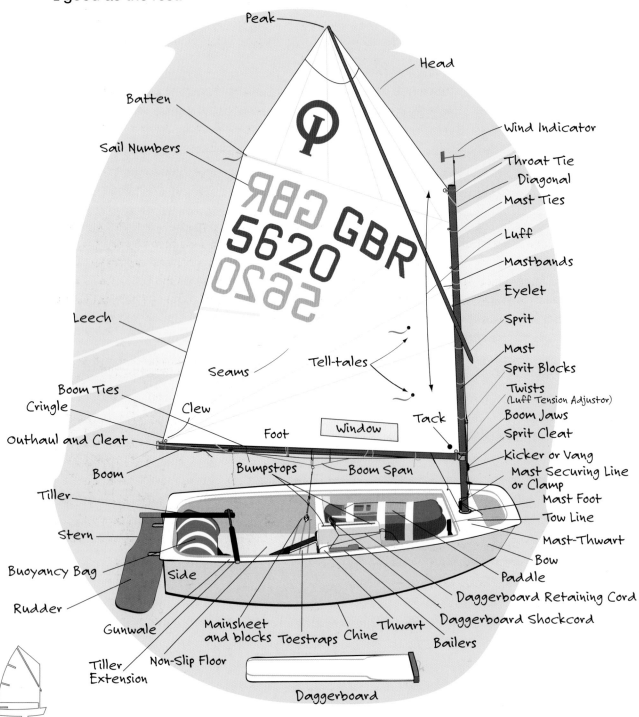

Peak
Head
Batten
Wind Indicator
Sail Numbers
Throat Tie
Diagonal
Mast Ties
Luff
Mastbands
Eyelet
Sprit
Leech
Mast
Sprit Blocks
Tell-tales
Twists
(Luff Tension Adjustor)
Seams
Boom Jaws
Boom Ties
Sprit Cleat
Cringle
Clew
Tack
Kicker or Vang
Foot
Window
Outhaul and Cleat
Mast Securing Line
or Clamp
Boom
Bumpstops
Boom Span
Mast Foot
Tiller
Tow Line
Mast-Thwart
Stern
Bow
Buoyancy Bag
Side
Paddle
Daggerboard Retaining Cord
Rudder
Daggerboard Shockcord
Gunwale
Mainsheet
and blocks
Toestraps
Chine
Thwart
Bailers
Tiller
Extension
Non-Slip Floor
Daggerboard

GBR
5620

SETTING UP THE BOAT

The Hull - IODA 95

All boats made after 1995 are almost identical in build so it is really important to look after your boat. Make sure you have a good trolley and keep your boat free from scratches which usually happen while launching or landing or if you are unlucky enough to have a collision! If you need to turn your boat over use two people, resting the gunwale on the trolley - half way over seems the easiest method.

If your hull does get scratched you can buy matching gel coat from boat builders and your repair will be almost invisible. Remember you don't need a new boat every year to do well. Provided you keep your boat in good condition there's no reason why it won't last a number of years.

Non-Slip Floor

The floor of the boat needs to be non slip or it's like standing on an ice skating rink and no amount of new sailing boots will solve the problem. If you have a new boat it is a good idea to wash the inside of the boat to degrease the floor and rub off any really sharp edges with some sand paper. To treat a well worn non-slip floor, you can mask off the floor with masking tape and re-finish the floor with specialist spray, or stipple on some gel coat with a cut off paint brush.

Daggerboard Case

Is quite wide and the Racing Rules (more about that later!) allow you to pad out the top and bottom using tape. The best tape to use is Jap tape which is available from chandlers. The next thing you need to do is to make sure rubber bump stops are fitted top and bottom of the case. This stops the daggerboard moving around and the edges getting damaged. Make sure that the bump stops meet smoothly with the bottom of the hull.

Spot the Jap tape and handle on the daggerboard case.

Daggerboard Retaining System

On different points of sailing, you need to control the position and height of the daggerboard. There are a variety of ways of doing this and which one to use is down to personal choice. The tension can be controlled by cord fed around the back of the daggerboard case to the shockcords on each side of the case. It is common to see a handle on the plastic tubing to enable the sailor to move the shock cord easily. See picture on page 13.

Mast Foot

There are two types of mast foot in general use, the pin and the cup. Both work well and need to be kept clean. If you want to you can lock off the mast foot so it can't move; you can either use a wing nut or a cam lock mast foot, to lock the mast step in position.

Sometimes the slider becomes loose; if this happens some thin plastic, in the groove, can be used to reduce the movement.

A cup mast foot.

Check to make sure that the mast foot is secured to the boat as they can come loose.

Mast collar

Some Oppy builders don't use mast collars on the bow thwart. For boats that do have them, the idea behind the mast collar is that it provides low friction. If one is fitted, then a low friction collar needs also to be fitted on the mast. Whenever you need to remove the collar be careful, it is oval in shape, longer fore and aft and narrower sideways and the shape must be kept. Check the mast collar bolts regularly because they can come undone.

SETTING UP THE BOAT

Mast Clamp

All Optimists need something to stop the mast falling out if the boat capsizes. The most common items used to stop this are; a mast tie on the bow thwart or, a mast clamp which is secured just underneath the thwart.

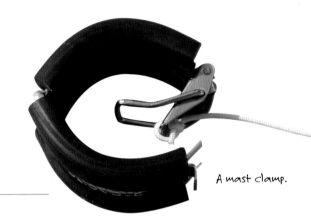

A mast clamp.

Toe Straps

Toe straps are really important for a young sailor. Ideally they should be padded and be adjustable so they can be adjusted to the correct length for the sailor. Usually there is either an eye under the rear buoyancy bag and the string can be adjusted to the correct length; or there are eyes in the toe straps allowing you to adjust the length.

Adjustable toe strap.

The straps need to be held up where they are attached to the thwart, to do this attach a shock cord to one strap and take it over the thwart, behind the daggerboard case and onto the other strap.

To prevent injuries while hiking there is no reason why you shouldn't adjust the lateral or sideways position of the straps on the midship thwart to get the straps in the right position for your leg length.

Buoyancy Bags

There are two types:

• PVC
• Fabric

Fabric bags appear to last longer. It is important with whatever type, they are not allowed to over inflate - otherwise when it is really hot the bags expand and the seams can burst!

Mainsheet Blocks

Two mainsheet blocks are secured to the hull, most are ball bearing blocks and after sailing they need rinsing in fresh water. The mainsheet block should be a lightweight, large diameter ratchet block, held up by a spring. Sometimes this spring is not flexible enough and will not allow the block to rotate smoothly so might need adjustment.

It is usually secured with a shackle and this can come undone, so it is a good idea to secure the pin with a cable tie. The smaller block is also secured to the hull. The boom block needs to be a lightweight ball bearing block.

Mainsheet blocks.

Mainsheet

There are two schools of thought, thick and thin sheets! In light weather or if the sailor is strong, a lightweight mainsheet of about 7mm is pretty good. In stronger winds lightweights or younger sailors might find a 9mm plus mainsheet is easier to control. It is a good idea to be able to take one purchase out of the mainsheet when the wind goes light. This reduces the mainsheet from 3:1 to 2:1, a lightweight snap shackle is ideal for this. Tapered mainsheets are also available and are a good alternative.

To reduce the length of the mainsheet, windage and weight, use a cord strop of 100mm to 150mm long between the top mainsheet block and the snap shackle.

Mainsheet attachment.

The mainsheet.

Mainsheet with snap shackle released.

SETTING UP THE BOAT

Towline

Every Optimist needs a buoyant towline 8 metres long and at least 5mm in diameter. Don't use the hole in the deck at the bow (drain hole) or you will damage your boat when you are being towed. Tie a bowline around the mast foot, coil up the line and stow under the deck at the bow or under one of the bow buoyancy bag straps.

- Make sure that the towline isn't passing through the small hole on the deck at the bow because this can damage the bow.

- Tie a loop in the towline about 1 metre from the mast foot.

- You can either tie another boat's towline to your loop or pass the towline through your loop and daisy chain a group of boats together.

- Some people like securing the next boat to their toe straps, but be careful because the towline can get caught around your rudder.

- RIBs often have purpose built towing systems so all you have to do is to clip the towline onto the loop in your towline.

Bailers

Optimist sailors need two bailers to keep the boat empty of water. Cut off 5 litre fuel cans are pretty good to use, one red and one green. Or buy ready made rectangular bailers from a chandler. A good option is to secure them with a continuous line or shock cord through the rear of the daggerboard case.

Bailers are essential.

Daggerboard and Rudder

The foils, as we call them have a very important function. Firstly both the rudder and daggerboard help to stop the boat from sliding sideways when sailing upwind and the rudder is also used for steering. Foils need to be looked after and kept away from strong direct sunlight to prevent warping.

There are two main types:

• Foam sheathed in glass and resin

• Varnished plywood

There are no real problems with either type, what is important is how stiff the foils are. Quite a lot of research has been carried out on foils and generally the stiffer the foils the better.

The result of new rules on tillers is that tillers are now aluminium and bolted to the rudder. Unfortunately they can and do work loose, so the use of self locking nuts and a liquid thread lock is recommended. Remember to check them regularly.

Tiller extensions should have a "golf style" grip and at the end of the extension a bobble or taped end which makes it easier to locate the end of the extension. We will see later this is very important.

The universal joint.

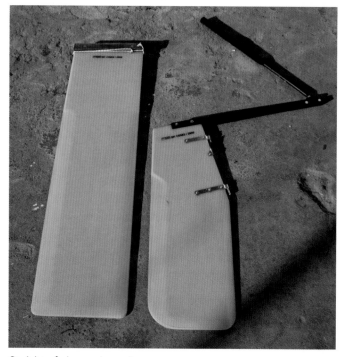

Rudder & daggerboard.

SETTING UP THE BOAT

Wind Indicator

A wind indicator at the top of the mast is essential because it tells you where the wind is coming from. There are two main types of wind indicator, flag or hawk type, both are pretty good, but be careful when rafted up and chatting as it is easy to hook each others' wind indicators off! The wind indicator fits into the top of the mast either through the holes in the pennant holders, or held in place by the diagonal and top mast ties.

A wind indicator.

Protest Flag on boom.

Protest Flag

In most events Optimist sailors are required to hail 'protest' and show a protest flag to protest another boat. Home made flags are acceptable or they are available from chandlers.

Paddle

You need to have a paddle, which can be secured by a lanyard under a buoyancy bag strap.

Class Rules

The IODA (International Optimist Dinghy Association), produces a set of international class rules to ensure that Optimist sailors are sailing a one design class and that it is a sailor's skill and ability that win races, not someone's ability to buy a newer or better boat.

Paddle held under buoyancy bag.

Measurement Certificate

If you are using an old boat, you probably won't have a measurement certificate. If you progress and decide to start racing, you will need a measurement certificate for your boat. The certificate proves that your boat meets all of the class rules. If you buy a second-hand boat and you are going to race, make sure you get the certificate from the previous owner. Remember each time you replace a major part such as a mast boom, sprit, sail, daggerboard or rudder, you will have to get it measured by a class measurer and signed off on your certificate.

Every year you will also need to have a buoyancy test on your boat to make sure your boat doesn't sink when it capsizes! A class measurer or club official will be able to organise this for you.

Keep a pencil in the boat so that when you finish a race you can write the numbers of the boats ahead and behind - just in case the finish boat misses you! Also handy if you are protesting, you can write the number of the other boat down.

Carry a whistle in your buoyancy aid.

Don't forget to carry spare sail ties looped around your buoyancy bag straps.

Argentinian Lucas Calabrese, Optimist Gold and Silver medalist at the Optimist Worlds.

The Sail

Provides the power to drive the boat forward. You are going to spend a lot of time looking at sails so it's important you know how the sail works so that you can get the best out of it in different conditions on the water.

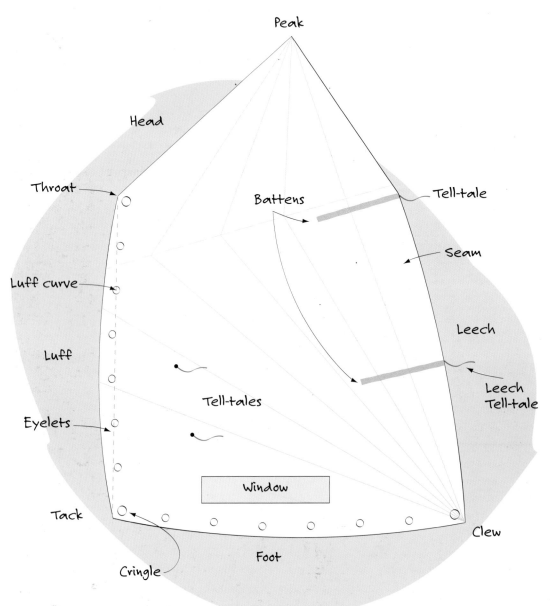

Optimist World Champion Wei Ni in China 305 relaxes before a race in the Asian games.

A Bit of Theory - Lift Off

Isn't it amazing how aeroplanes manage to take off? A plane takes off because the engines drive the plane forward and the shape of the wings lift the plane. Your boat's sails work just like an aeroplane's wing and as they fill with wind they develop something called lift and it's this lift you harness to drive your boat forward.

An aeroplane wing works by accelerating wind over the upper curved surface of the wing which reduces pressure. The wind is then slowed over the lower surface which increases pressure.

Diagram 1

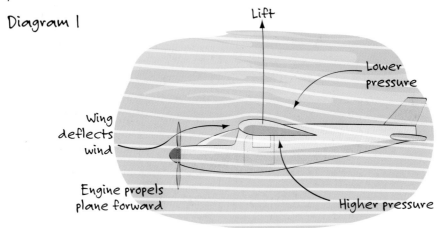

Diagram 2

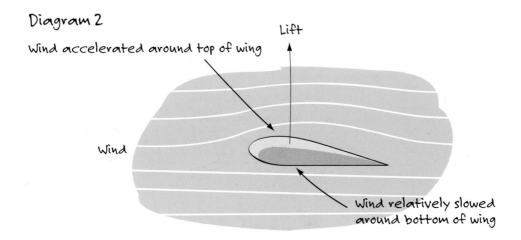

Pressure generally moves from low to high and as a result lift is created and the power generated in the wing makes it rise up into the air. Basically, a sail works in the same way but the sideways force you can see in diagram 3 shows how wind is converted into forward drive by the rudder, daggerboard and the shape of the hull. To make your sail work you sheet the sail in and deflect the wind around the sail and develop lift.

Diagram 3

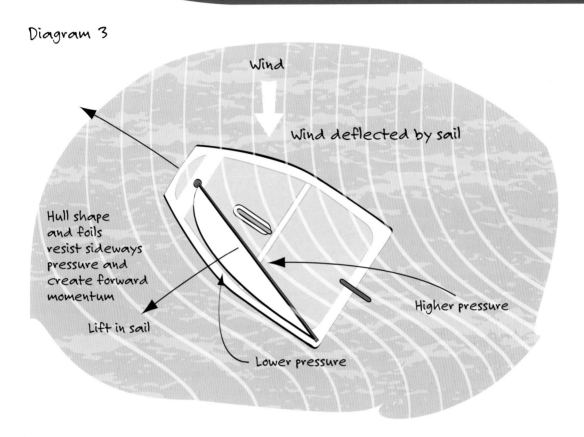

Wind

Wind deflected by sail

Hull shape
and foils
resist sideways
pressure and
create forward
momentum

Lift in sail

Higher pressure

Lower pressure

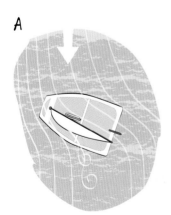

A

Sail oversheeted
and stalled – loses power

B

Sail undersheeted
– loses power

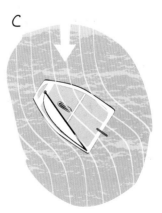

C

Sail set perfectly
using maximum power

Apparent Wind

If you are riding your bike on a day when there is no wind and you are riding at 5mph, you will feel a headwind of 5mph - this is apparent wind.

If you are riding your bike at 5mph and you have a tail wind (on your back) of 5mph you will not feel any apparent wind.

So what if the wind is coming from the side? Well that's a bit more tricky, basically as you accelerate the wind you feel on your face moves forward, and as you slow down the apparant wind moves back.

No wind, No speed = No apparent wind

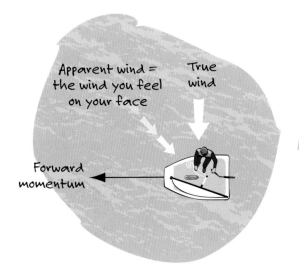

Apparent wind = the wind you feel on your face

True wind

Forward momentum

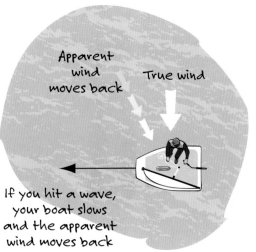

Apparent wind moves back

True wind

If you hit a wave, your boat slows and the apparent wind moves back

As you accelerate the apparent wind moves forward, as you slow down the apparent wind moves back

Camber, Draft and Chord

The curved shape of a sail is called camber and the depth is called draft (or fullness). We can make sails flatter or fuller depending upon whether we want more or less power. The chord is the length of the sail from the luff to the leech - which on an Optimist isn't very long.

Most sails work with a maximum draft at about 45% back from the luff, but as the wind increases the draft in the sail tries to move back, so we increase the luff tension to pull the draft forwards again.

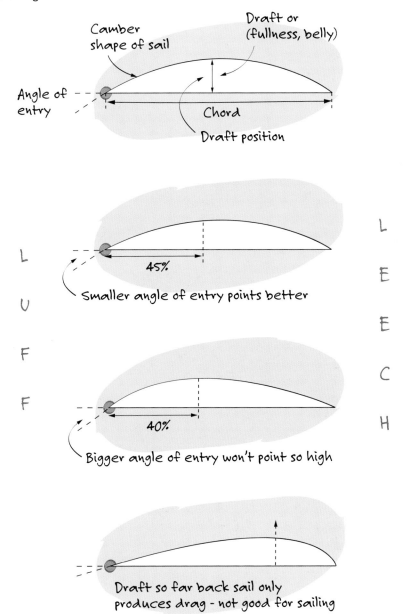

Camber shape of sail

Draft or (fullness, belly)

Angle of entry

Chord

Draft position

L
U
F
F

45%
Smaller angle of entry points better

40%
Bigger angle of entry won't point so high

Draft so far back sail only produces drag - not good for sailing

L
E
E
C
H

The Leech and Twist

The wind changes direction slightly and gets stronger the higher up the sail you go. This is due to there being less friction on the wind from the sail's surface. On an Optimist the shape of the leech is critical. The shape of the leech tells you how much twist you have in the sail. When sailing upwind the top batten when viewed from under the boom looking up, generally needs to be parallel with the boom (which isn't easy to do). If the top batten is hooked to windward, the sail will stall and the boat will sail slowly. If it points away from the boom you will be losing power and won't be able to point as high as other boats with correct twist.

Tell-tales

All sails need tell-tales – threads of wool attached to the sail. Tell-tales show us which way the wind is blowing as it flows past the sail. They are our wind eyes and it's essential that you learn to use them. You need surface tell-tales to help you point and give you a groove to sail in. Different sail makers put their surface tell-tales in different positions, from about 260mm to 310mm from the luff, and exit tell-tales on the leech close to the battens. The top leech tell-tale needs to be streaming 70% to 80% of the time, any less and the leech is too closed or hooked and any more and the sail is too open – it's all a question of balance! More on tell-tale use later in our Search for Speed (pages 83-85).

Racing can be very close so it's important to get your rig set up correctly.

Sails

The sail is the engine of your boat, but at the same time there is only so much a sailmaker can do to achieve optimum (the most) power in an Optimist sail. Sails fall into three categories, cross cut, radial and hybrids – which are cross cuts with radial heads and or radials with cross cut panels. Confused? Well read on.

- **Cross cut** - have a small number of panels. The sail tends to be flexible and can be adjusted across the wind range.

- **Radial** - have many more panels and the draft position tends to be locked in. They can be more difficult to read than cross cuts, but can also generate more power.

- **Hybrids** - have been designed to provide more readability into a radial sail and more shape and depth into the head of a cross cut sail. But when it's windy do you need a lot of power in the head of the sail?

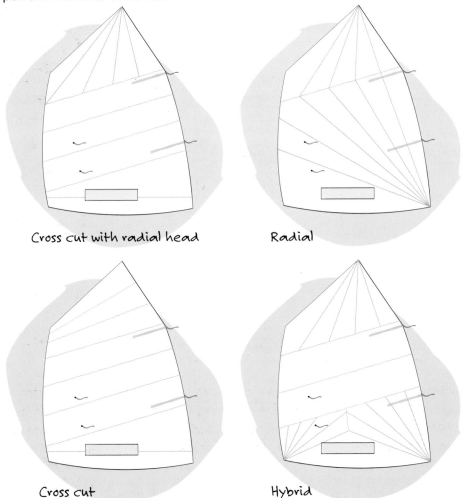

Cross cut with radial head   Radial

Cross cut   Hybrid

Sails are available in a variety of flat, medium and full cut versions and are cut sized for different weight sailors and conditions. There is no exact science as to which sail to use but as a guide here are some thoughts.

- **Flat cut** – suitable for younger and lightweight sailors (less than 35kg) and for sailing on flat waters because they offer more pointing ability.

- **Medium cu**t – for older, stronger sailors and also good for sailing on the sea where you need more power and less pointing. Good also for light sailors between 35kg and 40kg who are able to de-power the sail in a breeze.

- **Full cut** – generally for sailors over 50kg who are looking for as much power as they can find. The problem with fuller cut sails is that, because the chord length of the sail is quite short, it makes it very easy to stall, so they are more suited to experienced sailors.

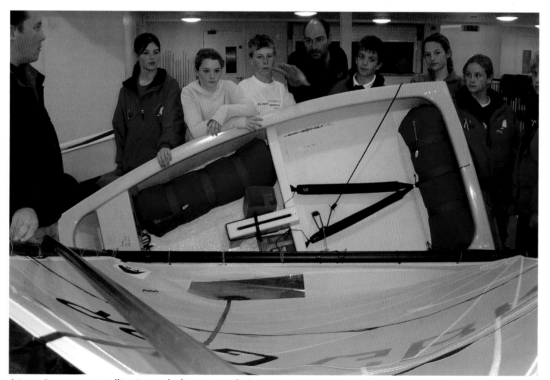

Adam Bowers and Ollie Green looking at sail shape with a group of sailors.

An important point is, that sailors using all designs of sails have won national, international and world championships, which proves that the skill of the sailor is more important than the type of sail. There is quite a lot of fashion involved in Optimist sails so look and see which sails are doing well in the national fleet and you won't go far wrong.

Luff Tension

Is always the subject of a lot of discussion. Luff tension controls the entry (see page 27) of the sail and determines its pointing ability. Mostly adjusted by increasing or decreasing the number of twists hooked over the pin stop on the mast.

A softer (slack) luff gives a flatter entry which is good for pointing ability on a lake and flat water. However on choppy water and sea sailing you need more power, so a firmer (tighter) luff gives a rounder entry and more power - but you can't point so high.

There is no exact method of luff tension and what is best varies from sail to sail, so really it comes down to the individual sailor's choice

Luff tension is controlled by the twists.

Checking out the luff tension.

Rigging the Sail

Tying the sail to the mast and boom would seem to be straightforward, but take care because the way you set the sail up on the mast and boom will have a direct impact on the sail's performance.

Basic Settings

The main sail ties, including the clew, tack and tack inhaul should be of 3mm pre-stretched cord. This is taken at least twice around the mast or boom and is long enough to tie a reef knot with an over hand knot to secure. The throat ties consist of one horizontal tie and one diagonal tie, and of 3mm cord. All other ties should be made of 1.5mm-2mm pre-stretched cord. Remember that the class rules only allow a maximum 10mm gap from the mast and boom to the sail. At least one championship has been lost because of a penalty for losing a sail tie!

Throat, Diagonal and Tack Ties

- The throat and diagonal ties are important because they set the throat of the sail and ensure that the sail sets within the bands on the mast.

- Throat and diagonal ties are usually tied externally with reef knots and half hitches to secure them.

- The tack has two tie's one on the boom and the other on the mast.

Throat and diagonal ties.

Sail set within the bands.

Tack ties on the mast & boom.

Sail Ties

The mast and boom sail ties need to be tied on very carefully. It is a good idea to tie and then glue the boom ties because most sailors roll their sails around the boom. Some sailors also set up their mast ties and then glue the knots so the sail can slide on and off the mast. Mast ties usually go once or twice around the mast and boom ties once. There can sometimes be some advantages in adjusting the sail ties to suit the conditions, so whether to glue the ties is up to you.

Careful adjustment of the mast sail ties makes it possible to increase or decrease the power in a sail by adjusting the luff curve to the shape of the mast, because your mast will bend while you are sailing.

Mast tie with reef knot finished off with half hitches.

Quick Set-up

If you don't want to be bothered fiddling with different settings for each sail tie, set them all the same distance - somewhere between 4-5mm off the mast works well.

Light Winds and Flat Water

The problem in light winds is that the mast doesn't bend very much. So to take some of the fullness out of the sail and allow the sail to point higher, you must ease the top mast and the tack inhaul by up to 6-7mm. Then gradually make the rest of the ties tighter – down to 2-3mm off the mast in the middle and have a soft luff.

Light Winds and Choppy Water

In these conditions, (which often exist on the sea) you want a powerful sail with the draft forward; so set the sail up as for the Quick Set-up (page 35) with a slightly firmer luff to pull the draft forward which provides more power.

Medium Winds

Generally, it is OK to set up the sail straight on the mast with all sail ties at an equal distance off the mast of 4-5mm.

Strong Winds

When the wind is strong, the mast will bend easily and, if we aren't careful we will end up with a sail which is too flat and with the fullness too far back. To retain some draft forward, tie the top and bottom mast ties tighter and ease the ties in the middle of the mast. This can look pretty ugly when on shore, but afloat the sail can work really well.

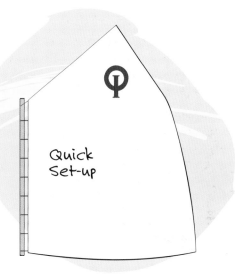

Quick Set-up

- All ties – 4-5mm off mast

Light Wind Set-up

- Top and bottom ties – 5-6mm off mast
- Middle ties – 2mm off mast

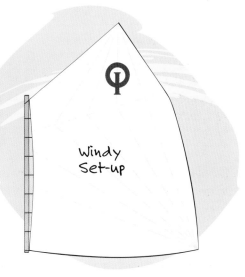

Windy Set-up

- Top and bottom ties – tight
- Middle ties – 4-5mm off mast

Kicking Strap (Vang)

The kicker's job is to control the height of the boom, help to lock in the shape of the sail and help to control the twist in the sail.

Sailing upwind in light to moderate conditions, the kicker needs to be a bit slack so that, as you sail downwind the boom doesn't rise too much allowing the leech to go forward of the mast, making your boat unstable. When it's windy, you will use a lot of kicker to control the sail shape' making it easier to sheet in and out in the upwind gusts and lulls: also stopping the leech when sailing downwind from going too far forward and causing your boat to death roll (see page 108).

Kicker On

If there are occasions when you need to put on a lot more kicker and there isn't anyone to help you try the following:

1. Ease your sprit.

2. Sheet in mega hard stepping or leaning forward and pulling your kicker tighter.

3. Ease the main and step or lean forward and put your sprit on again. Some sailors also like to pull the daggerboard up before putting the kicker on.

The Optimist kicker.

Adjusting your kicker on your own.

Outhaul and Cleat

The outhaul - is an important and often overlooked sail control. It controls the shape of the bottom third of the sail allowing it to be made fuller or flatter.

• Fuller = more power (except in very light winds).

• Flatter = reduces the power.

The cleat - used to adjust the outhaul. Now fitted on the starboard side of the boom so that it is easy to adjust.

Clew outhaul with tuning strip
to calibrate outhaul.

Outhaul cleat, note knot which stops
outhaul becoming too loose.

Spars

There are lots of different types and it is important to think through which will be best for you. If you look after your spars they should last a long time.

It is a myth that aluminium gets more flexible with use, it actually gets stiffer.

Mast

Most masts have similar bend characteristics, however, some manufacturers do produce stiffer masts. A stiff mast is fine for a heavier sailor, but the sail needs to be suitable for the mast bend characteristics. The sprit tackle is fitted on the front of the mast, with the cleat positioned generally in the low position so that you press down to tension the sprit. However, some sailors prefer to have the cleat in the higher position and pull down to tension the sprit. The choice is yours.

Sprit

The Optimist is one of the only racing sailboats with a sprit. Sprit tension is a really critical element in making an Oppy go fast. Its primary job is to control the leech tension, but it also helps to control the sail shape in the upper part of the sail. In light to moderate conditions the sprit should be tight enough to just take out the two creases in the sail just by the throat. As it gets progressively windier you will need more sprit. But a word of warning - don't overdo it, if the sprit is too tight when it is windy the sail will become unmanageable. If it gets really windy, a slightly bigger crease at the throat will help to reduce the power in the sail.

Sprit eased note creases at throat

Light wind setup.

Sprit tight no creases

Medium wind setup.

Sprit eased note creases at throat

Strong wind setup.

Booms

There are three main types of boom; narrow, regular and big booms.

• **Narrow booms -** bend too much and affect leech shape so they are rarely used by serious racers.

• **Regular booms -** of about 40 - 45mm are the most common and work well across the wind range, providing a good gust response.

• **Big booms -** of about 55mm are stiff, unforgiving and don't bend so much, but some bigger sailors like using them.

One thing that you should always check are the boom jaws, which should always fit tightly around the mast. If the jaws become loose, it is easy to replace them or use some tape around the mast as a temporary measure. Make sure that the mast and boom stay in line. If the mast and boom rotate out of sync with each other that can affect the entry of the sail.

A selection of booms at the Oppy Worlds.

Boom Span and Mainsheet Position

The boom span, (the rope beneath the boom), should be as tight as possible. If it's new don't trust the knots, re-tie them, they are known to come undone. If the boom span is tight you won't get caught on it every time you tack. The boom also has a plastic eye to tie the boom span depth adjuster. This is usually tied through the mainsheet ring on the boom span.

As you get bigger, you can move the boom span adjuster forward a bit to more above the thwart. This gives you much more room to tack without sinking the back of the boat.

Remember, the maximum boom span depth in the Rules is 100mm and 70-80mm is about right.

What Controls What?

If you think of the sail as two triangles, the kicker controls the bottom triangle, the sprit controls the top triangle of the sail and the mainsheet controls the sheeting angle and micro controls the leech tension.

B Sprit controls Area B

A Kicker controls Area A

Then Mainsheet controls whole rig

Boat Balance

Good boat balance is essential, and, as a rule of thumb, a well balanced boat is one which will head up gently into the wind when you let the tiller extension go while sailing upwind in flat water, and you are sailing the boat flat.

To understand what a balanced boat is, we need a little theory. First of all the hull of the boat has what we call a pivot point or centre of lateral resistance (CLR) and the sail has a centre of effort (CE), the theoretical pivot point of the sail.

• If the CE is above the CLR the boat should go in a straight line.

• If the CE is behind the CLR the boat will head up into the wind.

• If the CE is ahead of the CLR the boat will want to bear away from the wind. You can adjust the CE-CLR position by using mast rake.

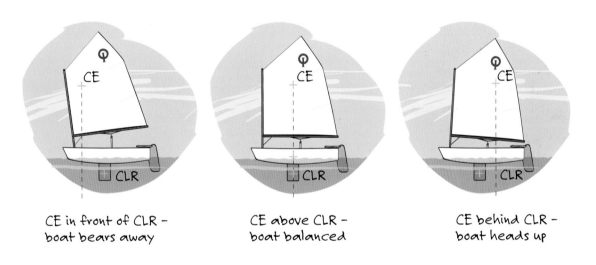

CE in front of CLR –
boat bears away

CE above CLR –
boat balanced

CE behind CLR –
boat heads up

Mast Rake

Mast rake is much talked about in the dinghy park and is one of the main ways of controlling boat balance. The challenge is to keep the boat balanced across the wind range and to do that we have several options.

A good way to measure mast rake is: without the kicker or sprit, using a steel tape, measure from the top of the mast to the top of the rear deck. Remember to measure it the same way each time you check it.

There is no reason why you shouldn't experiment with mast rake; but if you don't have the time the most effective mast rakes seem to be between 280cms and 284cms. Some radial sails like to be a little more upright in lighter winds and slightly further back in a breeze.

Hannah Mills finished fifth in the Optimist Worlds in Gran Canaria using 111-112 inches or 282-284cms which she hardly ever varied in her whole Optimist career. One day I had a phone call from her mother to say Hannah's boat was going 'pants' at a major event. I asked if they had checked the mast rake, there was a silence and after she checked it she found that Hannah's mast rake was way out. When it was adjusted Hannah won the next few races.

I spent a day with Croatian, Phillip Matika who was double World Optimist Champion. When he went afloat he would simply adjust his rig without a tape until it felt right. When we arrived back onshore I checked his mast rake and sure enough it was between 111-112 inches.

There is always some debate about mast rake for lighter and heavier sailors and it is an interesting point. Light weight sailors always heel a bit when sailing upwind in a breeze. This makes the boat want to head up, so it might make sense to rake the mast further forward, but this can result in problems of nose diving downwind. A solution is to pull up the daggerboard about 100mm to re-balance the boat, making the boat more controllable and not head up so much.

Brian Staite, a former GBR National Optimist Coach recommends that a horizontal boom when you are sheeted in is about right. The important message here is not to start fiddling with mast rake. If sailing performances could be better, it probably won't be the mast rake that makes the difference.

If you will sail mostly in summer conditions or are lucky enough to live in a warm climate a wetsuit will probably be enough to keep you warm. If you are going to sail in winter conditions you will need a drysuit and even in a northern European summer you might end up needing to wear a dry suit if you are out sailing for long periods.

Wetsuit Option

Most sailors now wear neoprene hiking shorts, with battened pads (to help hiking), and shoulder braces to stop them falling down around your ankles. A thermal top will keep you warm and a spray top will keep you dry.

Drysuit Option

Drysuits can be quite expensive, but there is a good second hand market (see boat jumbles or the internet). The latex seals need to be in good condition, talcum powder can prevent them from becoming sticky and make them easier to get over your hands and head. The seals can be cut to the wrist, neck and ankle size of the sailor. Some drysuits now use neoprene seals which are much more durable. If a latex seal breaks, use duck tape as a short term repair.

Drysuits have zips which need to be rubbed with wax or similar to keep them working smoothly. The most important thing with a drysuit is that, after you have put it on and zipped up, you have to vent the suit by squatting down and holding the neck seal open to let the excess air out. Under your drysuit you need to wear good thermal clothing like a fleece 'woolly bear'.

Other Kit

You need good footwear, neoprene boots are ideal and you will need a correct size buoyancy aid. Sailing gloves to help protect your hands and a cap to keep the sun off, or a fleece hat to keep you warm. Sunglasses are optional but sun cream is essential even on a cloudy day.

Name Your Kit

In a busy changing room it is easy to lose your kit so make sure you have marked everything with your name.

Sailing Bag

Really useful to have, especially one with a wet/dry compartment to stuff all of your kit into.

Drysuit & hats in the winter.

Cap, sunscreen and sunglasses in hot weather.

Alpine lake in the summer.

Drysuit.

Hikers & spraytop.

Cover up even in hot conditions.

Getting to grips with basic sailing

Sailmaker checking sail

At speed upwind in a decent wind

Section 2

'If you want to be amongst the best get out and practise'

Hannah Mills
Optimist Girls' World Champion
Women's 420 World Champion
470 sailor

Basic Sailing
Advanced Boat Handling
The Search for Speed
Mark Rounding

Before moving on to cover more advanced sailing techniques, for those of you new to Oppy sailing you need to read this section to help you with the basics. First we will have a look at some theory to help you understand what's going on.

Points of Sailing

The illustration will help you to understand the various points of sailing and your daggerboard position for each point.

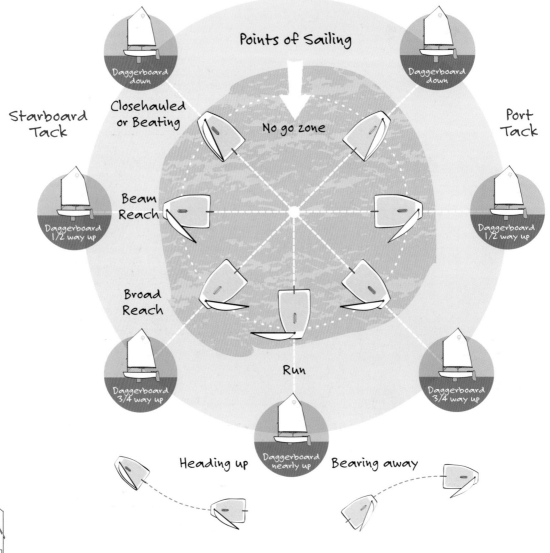

The Five Essentials

These were developed by Bob Bond, a GBR National Sailing Coach in the 1970s and are still in use today. So let's take a look at them.

Sail Setting   Making sure that your sail is always set correctly. Pull in until it stops flapping.

Balance   Sailing the boat upright.

Trim   Sit in the boat so that the bow isn't digging in and the stern isn't making big bubbles. Begin by sitting by the thwart when you are sailing.

Daggerboard
- Down for upwind unless windy then about 100mm up.
- Half way up on a reach.
- Three quarters up on a run (you can pull it up more as you get more experienced).
- You can mark your daggerboard with a permanent pen.

Course Sailed   There are a number of ways to get upwind, it depends upon the wind, tide, any obstructions and how many times you want to tack.

Sailing around a Course

This illustration shows you a simple course to sail around. You need to be able to:

- Sail upwind using different routes zig-zagging towards the wind.

- Tack and gybe when you need to.

- Head up and bear away.

- Sail on a reach and a run.

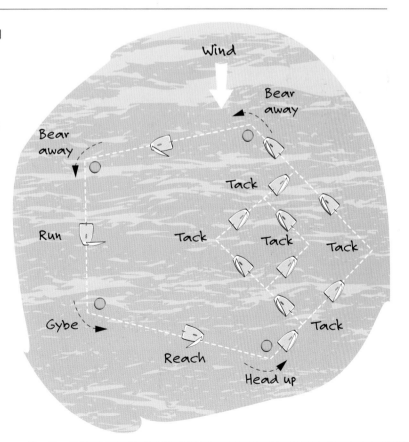

Land Drills

To get the basics right is great fun and essential to developing your skills quickly.

If you can leave your boat on its trolley and use tyres or buoys to support the boat then you will have the perfect platform to develop your skills.

First practise sitting on the side, then learn to sheet in with both hands, steering and then stopping by letting the mainsheet out without altering the rudder. Stand up and step forward (with the front foot) and push the boom out to stop your boat.

Practise hiking, tacking and gybing until it is second nature and you can do it with your eyes closed!

Land drills practice.

Practise sitting on the side.

Hiking, knees inside gunwale.

Hiking from behind.

Basic Tack

1) Push rudder to hold up.

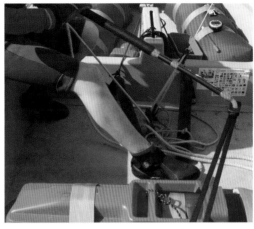

2) Step across, back foot first, duck under boom.

3) Sit down, shoulders forward.

4) Steer.

5) Swap hands.

6) Keep sailing.

Basic Gybe

1) Look where you are going.

2) Rudder towards you, stand up, step across, back foot first & duck under boom.

3) Centralise rudder.

4) Sit down and steer behind your back.

5) Swap hands.

6) Look where you are going.

Get a Grip

Most Optimist sailors use the dagger grip, thumb pointing towards the end of the extension when holding the tiller extension. A few sailors, but not many, in lighter conditions use the frying pan grip.

Sailor using the dagger grip.

Rigging and Launching

Rig your boat with the bow pointing into the wind. Whenever you are moving your boat around try to keep the wind coming from the bow to the back of the boat, otherwise the wind will fill the sail which will become unmanageable.

To stop your boat slipping off the trolley, make sure you tie your boat to the trolley.

Try to launch your boat with the bow pointing into the wind or you will make it amusing for everyone watching! If you are sailing in a group it's good to launch and recover in pairs.

1) Boat on trolley.

2) Push boat into water.

3) Hold boat head to wind.

4) Get a friend to help.

5) Rudder on.

6) Daggerboard in & off you go!

Start-Steer-Stop

When you go afloat, you'll start by sailing across the wind. Sit on the side of the boat opposite the sail, keep the rudder straight and pull the mainsail in. Now you are sailing across the wind.

If you get overpowered keep the rudder straight and let the mainsail out. To start off you can forget about the sprit, just tie the top of the sail neatly around the mast reducing the power in the sail.

Having loads of fun. Sprit taken off in windier conditions.

Steer

The next thing to learn is to steer while you are sailing. If you push the tiller gently away the boat will turn towards the wind, if you pull the tiller gently towards you the boat will turn away from the wind.

Stop

While you are sailing across the wind and you need to stop, let the mainsail out or, stand up and push the boom out turning your boat slightly towards the wind.

2) Step forward pushing the boom out to stop.

1) Ease mainsheet then stand up.

3) Then sit down again.

Tacking

How to turn your boat around by turning the bow through the wind - this is tacking.

- First check around to make sure it is safe to tack.

- While you are sailing across the wind turn the boat around by pushing the tiller extension gently away, turning your boat through the wind.

- Stay on the side, duck under the boom leading with your tiller extension – like Superman or Wonder Woman! Sit, getting your feet underneath you. Stand up and then step across the boat leading with your back foot.

- When the sail fills straighten the rudder and you will be sailing back to where you started from.

- Sit down on the new side (looking where you are going) and steering the tiller from behind your back.

- Swap hands and look where you are going.

1) Sailing along.

2) Push rudder, duck under boom.

3) Stand up.

4) Step across.

5) Sit down.

6) Swap hands, carry on.

Sailing Upwind

A real challenge is learning to sail towards the wind. If you point your boat straight into the wind the sail will act like a flag and eventually you will end up going backwards, not much fun – especially if you have an audience!

The closest you can sail to the wind is about 45 degrees. You will need to practise sailing a little closer to the wind than sailing across the wind. Turn your boat a little towards the wind and pull the sail in, to stop it from flapping.

Gradually you will be able to sail closer and closer to the wind until, with the sail pulled in, and the boom close to the corner of the boat, you will be sailing along the edge of what we call the no-go-zone. Because the wind is shifting around all of the time you have to keep checking to make sure that you are sailing as close to the wind as possible.

Once you have learnt this, you can now make progress upwind by zig-zagging your way upwind (see pages 59-60).

If you get overpowered when sailing upwind, ease your mainsheet to keep the boat flat, keep the rudder straight and let the sail out. Then if your boat sails into the no-go-zone and the sail starts to luff,bear away until the sail stops flapping. To do this needs a bit of anticipation, so if you see a darker gust of wind coming,ease your mainsheet before it gets to you. You can begin by sailing your boat with the daggerboard about 100-150mm up, making your boat easier to sail. If it is windy you can decide not to use the sprit which will reduce the power in the sail.

Perfect light wind technique sitting on the thwart.

Perching on the side looking ahead.

Tacking when Sailing Upwind

When you tack while sailing upwind, the tack is much quicker because you are only tacking through 90 degrees. To tack sailing upwind, check that it is clear for you to tack, be positive and lead with your tiller extension. If you get overpowered or are a little slow crossing the boat, ease the mainsheet as you cross the boat. Don't forget to straighten the rudder as soon as the boom comes over your head and step across, sit down, steer, swap hands and after you have tacked look where you are going. This will take lots of practice, but it's worth it.

1) Sailing close hauled.

2) Head up using rudder and lean in.

3) Duck under boom.

4) Step across and centralise tiller.

5) Steer with hands behind your back.

6) Swap hands, carry on.

Sailing on a Reach

Sailing on a reach in light to moderate conditions is straightforward. All you do is let the sail out until it just starts flapping, then pull it in again (until it just stops flapping) then pull up the daggerboard to about half way up.

Broad reach sail three quarters of the way out, daggerboard half to three quarters up.

Sailing on a Run

If you are sailing on a beam reach (across the wind) and you want to sail on a run, you need to pull your daggerboard to about three quarters up, then pull the tiller gently towards you. At the same time ease your mainsheet about three quarters of the way out. Eventually your wind indicator will be pointing towards the back of your boat and you will be running before the wind.

Remember, if the boat becomes a bit unstable, pull the sail in a little and the boat will settle down again.

Sailing on a run - main out to 90° and daggerboard up.

Heading Up and Bearing Away

Next we'll take a look at two essential skills to help you manoeuvre your boat around a mark.

Bearing Away on a Run

When sailing upwind and you want to bear away round a mark onto a run:

1 Approach the mark close hauled.

2 Ease your mainsheet and pull the tiller towards you.

3 Pull the daggerboard three quarters up.

4 Let the sail out no more than 90 degrees.

If it's windy – don't let the mainsheet out too far and your boat will be more stable.

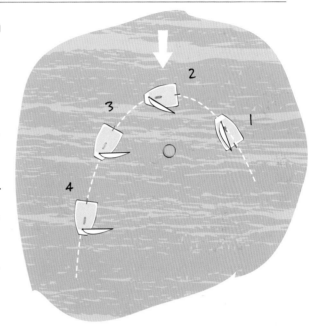

Heading Up to Close Hauled

When sailing downwind on a run and you want to head up around a mark:

1 Approach the mark.

2 Daggerboard down.

3 Push the tiller gently away and sheet in as you turn.

4/5 You are now close hauled.

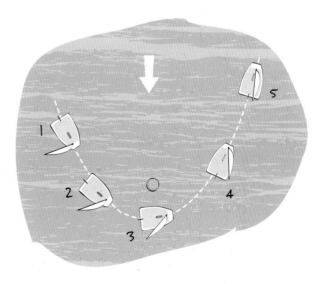

Gybing

Good news, gybing in light winds in an Optimist is easier than tacking! We will now go through the steps which will lead to a successful gybe.

- Pull in a couple or armfuls of mainsheet so the boom isn't quite at 90 degrees.

- Gently pull the tiller extension towards you, the boat will now turn away from the wind.

- Lean in and grab the falls of the mainsheet and pull towards you.

- Duck under the boom as it comes across your head, with your feet underneath you.

- Stand up and step across the boat leading with your back foot.

- Straighten the rudder as you cross the boat leading with your tiller extension.

- Sit down on the new side, swap hands and look where you are going.

1) Steering boat, sheet in a little.

2) Rudder forward, grab falls of mainsheet and pull.

3) Duck under the boom.

4) Step across, sit down, steer & swap hands.

Returning to the Shore

As you come towards the shore you will need to slow down. Point your boat into the wind, pull the daggerboard up and hop out into the shallow water taking care not to catch your rudder on the bottom - sounds easy but takes some practice.

Working with a partner, get your trolley ready. Then, holding the bow of your boat into the wind, secure the boat to the trolley. Take your boat out of the water keeping the bow pointing into the wind. If you are coming to a jetty or pontoon, come in towards the wind and slow down stylishly. Get someone to hold your boat while you put the rudder and daggerboard in.

Working in pairs makes landing easier.

Capsize

Capsizing is a natural part of sailing, overbalance and you capsize. Don't forget to acknowledge the crowd if there is one - smile and wave!

If the boat has gone right over, grab the daggerboard and climb onto the hull of the boat.

Right the boat towards the wind and gradually the boat will come up. If you are a lightweight you might have to climb onto the daggerboard when the boat is half way up to help get the mast out of the water.

When the boat comes upright climb in and start bailing like mad!

1) Oops... I've capsized!

2) Get to the windward side of the boat/

3) Grab the daggerboard and right the boat.

4) Grab the gunwale.

5) Take a breath.

6) Climb in quickly.

7) Get in and stand up.

8) Get bailing and remember to smile!

Now let's take a look at the boat handling skills you need to get around the race course. There is no doubt that hours practising boat handling skills will pay off. It's all about using the best techniques and practising them until they are second nature for all the varying conditions you will sail in. As you practise and progress your sailing will develop. Techniques which suit your size, experience and skill may differ from those we show in this book. It is all down to what suits you best.

Before going on to look at particular skills let's take a look at the elements which drive and turn an Optimist. To do this we use a combination of the wind, the sail, the body and heeling the boat. Each of these creates energy which is used to turn the boat. You can alter the effects of each element by the use of speed, timing, acceleration, control and positioning. You need to learn to become accurate and consistent and finally to develop feel – so that your boat handling becomes automatic. When this happens you can spend most of your time getting yourself around the race course.

To develop good boat handling skills you need to learn:

• To transfer your weight around the boat.

• How to shift or transfer your centre of gravity.

• How to balance from one leg to the other.

• Be able to transfer your weight onto one leg, making it easy to move your other leg.

Using The Sail To Turn The Boat

Generally if you sheet in, the boat will want to turn towards the wind, and if you sheet out the boat will want to bear away.

Practise standing on one leg!

Using Heel To Turn The Boat

Heel the boat to windward and it will want to bear away and heel it to leeward, it will want to head up.

Heel to windward to bear away.

Heel to leeward to headup.

Equal And Opposite Actions – Creating The Force

Now for a little experiment. Get a dried pea, bean or a pencil, place it between the end of your finger and thumb, squeeze it – it will fly away from you. Squeeze it very hard and it goes a long way. Don't squeeze it as hard and it will just fall to the ground. This is the force. It is about using opposites to create energy. We use this sort of energy to sail a boat when tacking and especially accelerating. Anyway, enough of that Newtonian stuff about actions and reactions – read on…

Techniques and Skills

We all mix up these two words and their meanings, so what do they really mean?

Technique - The physical movements that make up a manoeuvre, like a tack, or a gybe.

Pressure - Putting your technique under pressure by doing it faster, longer, when you are distracted, or while you are trying to work out new priorities.

Skill - The ability to tack and gybe.

Skilful - The ability to tack or gybe to a high standard, consistently in varying conditions while under pressure - as in a race.

Technique + Pressure = Skill

All the techniques we will look at are a bit complicated and, on the basis that you can't eat an elephant whole because you get indigestion, we are going to break the techniques down into easily digestible chunks. It is then possible to work on the individual components or processes and put them together smoothly and automatically.

You can't eat an elephant whole or you get indigestion – you need to break it down into small digestible chunks. That's why we break sailing skills down into digestible chunks!

Most sailing manoeuvres can be broken down into three phases.
Entry – Mid Phase – Exit. This can be a really helpful way of developing your skills.

Tacking

You need to be able to roll tack an Optimist well in all conditions, whether on flat water or in waves. There are a number of tacking variations you can develop:

- Step tack

- Fast step

- Hop

- Hop off the daggerboard case

- Tacking to sitting in

- Tacking from sitting in, to sitting out

- Strap to strap tacking

The Rules say you can't come out of a tack faster than you went into it, but that doesn't stop you from tacking as efficiently as possible.

Developing great technique takes a lot of practice.

Light Wind Tack

The aim is to roll tack smoothly using as little rudder as possible. Make sure you are sailing as fast as possible.

1) Sailing close hauled.

2) Head up.

You will probably be sitting in on the thwart. Heel the boat to leeward to make it head up and at the same time use some rudder to help the turn. As the boat heads up (2) squeeze the mainsheet slightly which will help the boat head up.

3) Head to wind.

4) Roll the boat ducking under the boom.

Then, pause until the boat comes up to head to wind (3), then just as the sail backs, sit up onto the gunwale, knees slightly pointing forward and roll the boat to windward. Duck under the boom (4), pause for a moment, feet underneath you, ease the mainsheet, centralize the rudder, stand and step across the boat leading with the back foot and the tiller extension. Sit well forward, turn your shoulders towards the bow, steer, and squeeze the mainsheet.

5) Steer then swap hands.

Swap hands and when you are comfortable, look where you are going and carry on (5). You might find it difficult to swap hands behind your back in the light stuff so try to swap hands by either leaning well forward or by taking the tiller extension with an underhand grip close to the tiller (6).
This results in minimum rudder movement. There are other methods and it's up to you to experiment.

Sounds difficult but with practice, you will be able to do it with your eyes closed!

As the wind increases and you start to perch on the edge of the gunwale, to head up lean in (possibly lifting your bottom off the gunwale), then as the boat gets to head to wind, sit back down and use your momentum to roll the boat.

6) Steer with hand behind back, use under hand grip to swap position.

7) Steering with backhand on the base of the tiller extension.

A light wind alternative to swap hands, is to take the tiller extension with the new backhand using the underhand grip.

Make sure you sit forward and your shoulders are pointing forwards out of the tack after you sit down. It is easier to steer before swapping hands.

Medium Wind Tack

In medium winds you need to roll tack smoothly, to achive this:

1 Have plenty of speed into the tack.
2 Lean in and use some rudder.
3 Squeeze the mainsheet slightly.
4 Pause until head to wind.
5 Knees forward.
5 Roll the boat to windward.
7 Duck under the boom, leading with your tiller extension hand.

8 Cross the boat, back foot first.
9 Ease the sheet.
10 Centralise the rudder.
11 Sit forward, shoulders forward, squeeze the mainsheet.
12 Swap hands.
13 Sail away.

Smaller sailors may have to dump more mainsheet to balance the boat. Heavy sailors need control of their weight, so that they don't land too heavily on the new windward side.

1) Sailing fast, check ahead.

2) Head up, lean in, use some rudder.

3) Head to wind, duck under boom.

4) Cross the boat.

5) Swap hands.

6) Sail away.

Strong Wind Tack

You need to tack much flatter and to control the power in the sail.

- You will be fully hiking.
- Keep the boat flat, heavier sailors need to sit slightly further back in the boat.
- Steer up to head to wind, easing the mainsheet just before head to wind.
- Jab rudder, duck under the boom and explode across the boat leading with the tiller extension.
- Hop or jump into the toestraps, hike hard and when ready swap hands.
- Sail away.

1) Sail fast, hiking.

2) Duck and cross the boat.

3) Hike.

4) Swap hands.

5) Sail away.

Stuck in Irons — Head to Wind

To avoid going head to wind when it's windy and you are tacking, make sure the boat bears away enough out of the tack. You can do this by making sure you ease the mainsheet out of the tack. In a strong gust, by a bit of anticipation, you can avoid being forced head to wind by anticipating it and easing your mainsheet before the gust hits you.

If you find yourself head to wind (which you will), use the following to get you out of trouble:

• Ease the mainsheet, pull the daggerboard half way up and push the boom out.

• Sit on the side, hike out, sheet in slightly and your boat will get going again.

Light to Medium Wind — Choppy Water

The aim with this tack is to keep your speed up but don't point too high. Time your tack so that you are heading up down the back of a wave and that you tack on the top of the next wave. Use a little more rudder to get the boat through the wind faster.

Strong Wind — Choppy Water

No longer roll tacking (you don't want to fill up or lose control), the aim here is to tack in an area of flatter water. Look ahead and if possible wait, then jab the rudder to get the boat quicker through the tack. You need to go from hiking to hiking, so get through the tack quickly and dump the mainsheet a bit. Half way through the tack, hike strap-to-strap, hike hard, swap hands and sheet in again after the tack.

Exiting the Tack

The angle you exit the tack is important:

• Too high and you will lose power.

• Too low and you will stall.

So practise controlling the angle of your exit.

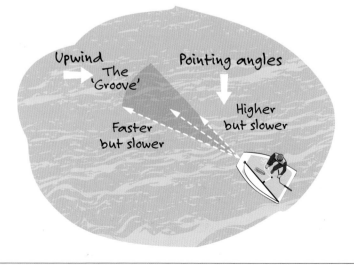

Gybing

Just like tacking your gybing must be technically correct and well practised.

In light winds you can roll gybe, the aim is to ensure that you come out of the gybe as fast as you were sailing when you went into the gybe. You need to think about the angle you will come out of the gybe. Again, just like with tacking, think about the entry – mid phase and exit of the gybe.

Light Wind Gybe

Needs to be smooth to keep the boat moving. The photographs show you the parts of a successful gybe.

Remember the more you practise the better you will get.

1) Sheet in a little and steer gently into the gybe.

2) Sit on the side grabbing falls of mainsheet.

3) Pull the sail over your head rolling the boat towards you, keep the rudder straight.

4) Leading with tiller extension, step lightly across the boat leading with your back foot.

5) Sit down and swap hands.

Medium Wind Gybe

As the wind increases you will need to concentrate and keep control of your boat while you are gybing.

1) Sheet in slightly, bear away and grab falls of the mainsheet.

2) Pull the mainsheet, duck as boom crosses.

3) Fast step or hop across and sit down.

4) Shoulders forward and steer.

5) Swap hands and sail away.

1) Sail fast on a run.

2) As the boom moves leap across the boat.

3) Sit down and swap hands.

4) Smile!

Strong Wind Gybe

Good technique and plenty of practice will make sure that you have a reliable strong wind gybe.

The key points are:

A. Make sure you are in control and the boat is stable on a run.

B. Bear away steering positively and sheet in a little.

C. Grab the falls of the mainsheet and pull hard.

D. When the boom moves, leap across the boat centralising the rudder.

E. Sit down and when ready swap hands.

F. Smile.

or alternatively from B above:

- Stand up taking a small step across with your front foot.

- Step across with your back foot, keeping the boat flat and balanced.

- Grab the falls of the mainsheet and pull hard.

- When the boom moves, step across the boat centralising the rudder.

- Sit down and when ready swap hands.

- Smile.

Gybing in Waves

The aim is to try to gybe going as fast as possible down the face of the wave. The apparent wind will move forward and the power in the sail reduces. The key to gybing in waves is timing, and, getting your timing right, it just takes lots of practice (that word again!). The plan is to gybe when the boat is surfing down a wave, when the power in the mainsheet suddenly becomes lighter, and there is least pressure on the sail.

1) Steer accurately and pick up the wave.

2) Surf down the wave staying on the steepest section of the wave.

3) Enjoy the speed and get ready to gybe.

4) When you are going as fast as possible bear away, and sheet in a little.

5) Pull hard on the mainsheet, duck under the boom and bounce across the boat.

6) Sit down, steer, then swap hands and smile.

Wheelbarrow Turn

That's what Thomas Mallandine, 2 times GBR Optimist Champion and ISAF Bronze Medallist in the 420 called it. Instead of gybing when it's really windy you can tack round, bear away and carry on sailing. Thomas did just that to become the GBR 420 Youth Champion when it was so windy that dogs were being blown off their leads!

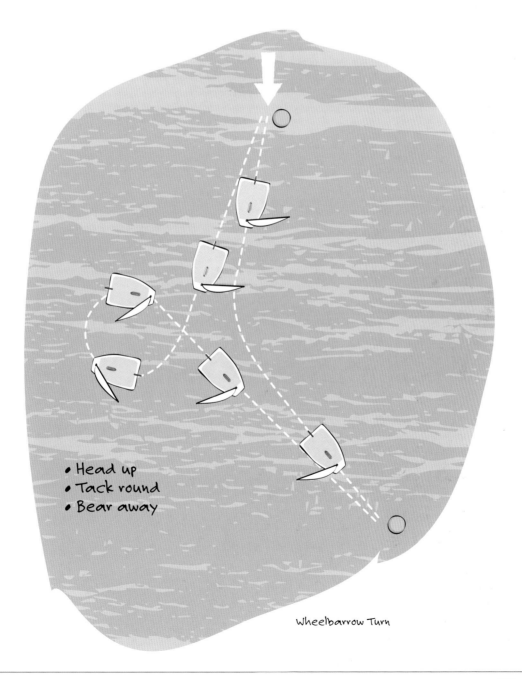

- Head up
- Tack round
- Bear away

Wheelbarrow Turn

One and Two Turns Penalties

You need to be confident that you can complete a One and Two Turns Penalty anywhere around the course because both are used as penalties. The One Turn Penalty is for hitting a mark and a Two Turn Penalty for a boat on boat infringement or a Rule 42 jury penalty. It is possible to complete a One Turn Penalty in 7 seconds and a Two Turns Penalty in 14 seconds.

The rules require you to complete the turns in the same direction. Whether you start a turn with a tack or a gybe, really depends on where you are when you start your turn. If you are sailing upwind it's often easier to tack first and if sailing downwind gybe first, but it isn't always that simple. Make sure you keep out of the way of other boats whilst completing a penalty as you have no rights. After the first tack or gybe a lot of top sailors let go of the tiller extension and use a lot of mainsheet and body weight to spin the boat around. They usually grab hold of the tiller extension again to complete the final tack or bear away.

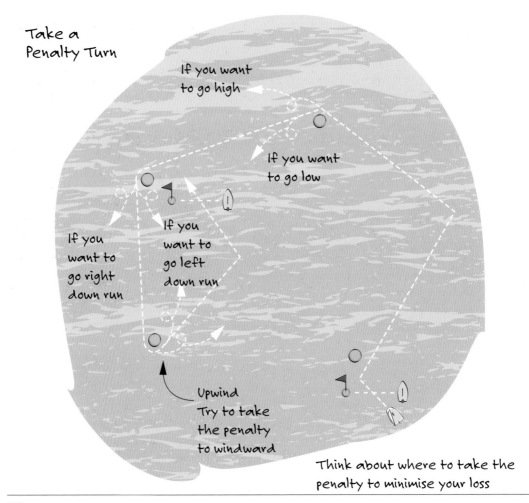

Take a Penalty Turn

If you want to go high

If you want to go low

If you want to go right down run

If you want to go left down run

Upwind
Try to take the penalty to windward

Think about where to take the penalty to minimise your loss

ADVANCED BOAT HANDLING

One Turn Penalty

1) Make sure you are in control.

2) Gybe - you can let go of the tiller extension.

3) Grab the extension.

4) Tack.

5) Bear away.

6) Sail away.

Remember you have to complete a penalty as soon as possible. Get out of the way of other boats as you have no rights when you are completing your turns. To minimise your loss think about where the best place might be to take your penalty.

Great boat speed makes you something of a tactical genius and the ability to sail fast isn't rocket science, it just takes a lot of practice. So let's take a look at the skills you need to develop great boat speed.

Upwind Speed

When you are sailing upwind the breeze is never constant and as well as the bigger shifts there are always smaller gusts, lulls and fluctuations.

The fastest Optimist sailors will always be making micro adjustments to get the best out of these ever changing conditions, the aim being to keep a high average boat speed.

Mainsheet tension is very important, all too often the mainsheet is neglected and as a result you can be sheeted in too hard. The result will be the boat stalls, your main is too far out, you have no power and can't point. You need to get used to easing and squeezing your mainsheet in the gusts and lulls. We are not talking about huge amounts, just three clicks, five clicks and ten clicks on your ratchet, always looking at the effect on your leech shape, boat speed, pointing and tell-tales.

- Steer very accurately and use as little rudder as possible. One way of doing this is, to put the hand holding the tiller extension on your thigh, then when you lean in and out to balance the boat, you won't end up moving your tiller. When sailing in waves you need to use more rudder – more about that later.

- Learn to steer using body weight, lean out to bear away and lean in to head up.

- Be proactive to gusts and lulls, see them coming on the water. In gusts, provided they don't overpower you, you can sit out and sheet in more. When the lull comes you need to sit in and ease the main slightly.

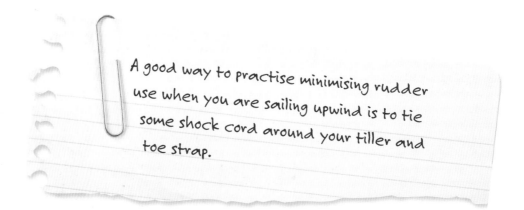

A good way to practise minimising rudder use when you are sailing upwind is to tie some shock cord around your tiller and toe strap.

Tell-tales

Tell-tales are essential, they are your wind eyes, because they give you visual information about the wind flow over your sail. There are two types of tell-tales:

• Surface tell-tales which are on the surface of the sail.

• Exit tell-tales on the leech of your sail.

Surface Tell-tales

Surface tell-tales help you sail upwind. You can use them to sail in a sort of groove – between sailing fast and free and pointing high.

Tell-tales are your wind eyes, learn how to use them.

Upwind

Surface tell-tales are generally set between 260-310mm back from the luff. The position of surface tell-tales can be significant because:

- If they are too far forward, to get them flowing horizontally, you won't be able to point high.

- If they are too far back and they are flowing, you won't be pointing high enough.

- If both surface tell-tales are flowing horizontally backwards, you have flow over both sides of the sail but you aren't pointing very high.

- If the leeward tell-tale is horizontal and windward tell-tale is pointing up slightly, then you are pointing quite high.

If the leeward tell-tale is pointing down you have a problem and need to either head up or ease your mainsheet to get flow over the sail again.

The wind flow over the top tell-tale is often disrupted by the sprit when on starboard tack.

Reaching

When sailing on a reach the easiest way to set your sail is, to ease the mainsheet until the luff just starts to flap and then pull the sail in a little. A more refined way is to keep the leeward tell-tale flying horizontally, if it drops, ease the mainsheet until it flies horizontally again.

Running

Surface tell-tales don't really work on an Oppy when sailing on a run, so don't worry about them, you just need to use your leech tell-tales instead.

Top Tip
If you spray your tell-tales with silicone spray they will carry on working even when wet.

THE SEARCH FOR SPEED

Leech Tell-tales

Leech tell-tales are really useful for Oppy sailors, they give you a lot of information about the shape of your leech. The shape of the leech is controlled mainly by a combination of kicker and sprit tension and in lighter winds by mainsheet tension.

Upwind

Your leech shape will affect your power, pointing and speed. Let's take a look at how this happens:

• All tell-tales streaming and leech open – good for light airs and when it's windy.

• Top tell-tale flying 70-80% of the time – good for pointing.

If the top tell-tale is pointing down or around the back of the sail, it is telling you that your leech is hooked or stalled and that your boat will slow down dramatically. You can often see the top batten pointing to windward. The solution is to ease the main maybe only a couple of centimetres and the top leech tell-tale will fly again. Aim to keep the top batten parallel with the boom – in light winds you might also need to ease the sprit a little.

Downwind

The leech tell-tales are also useful on a run, ideally we want to keep them streaming. To achieve this in light to moderate winds you need to learn to ease your sprit on the run to open the leech, this is tricky for smaller sailors who should leave their sprits alone.

Balancing the Boat

The position you sit in needs a lot of thought and the bigger you get the more significant it is. Lightweights can sit almost anywhere and get away with it, but as you grow bigger you can't sit in the positions which you used to sit in when you were smaller.

Light Winds

This requires the most awkward sitting position to get into, easy for small sailors but demanding if you are bigger.

The aim is, to keep the boat upright or slightly heeled to leeward, and to keep the boat trimmed so that both ends are just out of the water. This gives maximum waterline length and minimises drag. The one thing you don't want to do is, to have your weight too far back or the transom will dig in creating lots of turbulence and bubbles and your boat will sail slowly.

If you are a lightweight, you can sit on the thwart and if bigger you can kneel with one knee either side of the mainsheet. Although difficult to do it does work! You can even experiment with sitting on your bailer!

Sitting on thwart looking forward.

Bigger sailors often sit like this!

Various light wind sitting positions.

Transition from Light to Medium Winds

The transition from light to medium winds is interesting and many sailors hike out too early. As the wind increases, lighter sailors can perch on the side and heavier sailors can sit on the thwart leaning out in the gusts. As it gets windier, heavier sailors perch their bottoms just on the inside of the gunwale, feet flat on the floor under the toe strap. Then as a gust comes, lean out to balance the boat and only when the wind starts to increase should you sit further out.

You need to work on sit up tall, bottom in, shoulders out, until you are fully hiked - this is super fast.

Avoid the 'bumble bee back', where your back is curved forward towards the sail and your head is leaning in.

With the transition from medium to light winds move your weight in earlier than you think, it stops the boat heeling on top of you and bearing away too much.

Tell-tales streaming off

ESP

Perching on the gunwale, perfect technique.

Hiking Your Boat

When sailing, it is important to be locked into your boat so that if you are using your body to get through waves, any action through your shoulders is transferred through the gunwale and your feet, to the toe straps and then to the boat. If you are sailing in waves and you are locked in and you lean towards the back of the boat, the bow will rise over the wave preventing your bow from bashing into the wave; thus slowing you down and smoothing out the boat's motion through the water.

In lighter winds you can jam your front foot under the front of the strap and your back foot underneath you locking you into the boat.

As is gets windier, both feet need to be hooked under the straps, try not to point your toes like a ballet dancer as it stretches your tendons. Just keep your feet close together not pointing in or out, just pointing up. Keep your knees close together, unless it gets really windy when placing your feet slightly further apart will give a bit more balance.

Your Upper Body

Even if you are sailing in small waves, your boat tends to accelerate and decelerate as you sail along. You might notice that as your bow goes up or hits a wave, your upper body rocks forward. It's very slow and to combat this rocking forward:

- Sail with your shoulders angled slightly towards the back of your boat.

- Hold your mainsheet arm up in a "chicken wing" position. It helps to stop you rocking forward as well as giving you a powerful position to sheet in and out from.

- Sit up tall and not like a bumble bee.

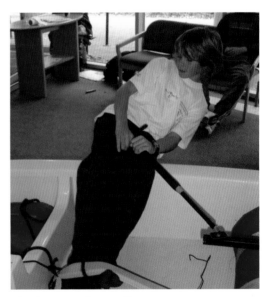

Shoulders back - small waves.

Medium Winds

Light sailors will be sitting on the side and hiking, bigger sailors will be on the side, feet under the toe strap with feet on the floor.

Toe strap length is important and it is essential not to hike off your knees. This means that your knees shouldn't be directly over the gunwale, your knee joint will just lever open. You should be positioned so that your knees are just inside the gunwale.

Knees inside gunwale.

Good hiking position in medium winds.

Don't Forget To Sit Up Tall

Good posture is essential while you are sailing and will help you with the long term health of your back. If you have good posture you will be:

• More comfortable while you are sailing.

• Able to turn your shoulders and head further.

• Able to see further.

• Have better hiking.

Sit up tall

Bumble bee back

Strong Winds or Fully Hiking

Make sure your toe straps are the right length. If you are a bigger sailor, sit slightly further back in the boat to stop the bow slapping into waves. Keep your feet forward so you are sitting in a slightly diagonal position. If you are a smaller sailor you can probably remain in your usual sailing position. You need to learn to hike for long periods of time. To start with you will find that you can only hike maxed out for a short period and have to shuffle your bottom in. As your fitness develops you will find that you can hike for longer and longer. Fitness training to develop your tummy muscles and thighs is essential (see page 244).

Shoulders back to avoid hitting waves.

Powerful hiking in strong winds.

- When hiking for long periods on one tack learn to rest each leg by taking the weight off one leg and then off the other.

- Try not to over arch your back when you are sailing, you may flat hike for short periods but most of the time you will be upright to about 45 degrees back.

Excellent hiking technique, taller sailor using both toestraps.

Top Tip
Bigger sailors often hike using both toe straps because they have longer legs!

4 Zones of Concentration

While sailing you need to be able to focus on four different zones that affect your sailing:

- **Me -** This is all about 'Me' and how are you feeling. Are you focused, stressed, anxious, had enough to drink and eat? How are you adjusting the mainsheet? Are you holding the tiller extension too tight?

- **Now -** This is all about what is happening now and where you are. Is your rig set up correctly for the conditions? Are you sailing fast? Are you over sheeted or under sheeted? What about the next wave, the gust you're dealing with or the boat right next to you? Are your tell-tales flowing?

- **Next -** Looking further away from your boat, the next shift, the next group of boats or a mark rounding.

- **BigP -** This is all about where the fleet is? What the tide is doing? Is there more wind on one side of the course? Does that headland affect the wind? Or, what about that big black cloud and so on?

It's all about avoiding distractions, focusing and getting your priorities right.

The 4 Zones of Concentration

Sailing upwind – the 'Pizza Zone'

Combined with the 4 Zones of Concentration, when sailing upwind, the area where most of the information you need to help you comes from is what I call the 'Pizza Zone'. It looks like a slice of pizza, from dead ahead to about 90 degrees.

One famous Oppy sailor was so fast that he spent too much time looking back at what was going on behind, he missed some whopping big shifts. His dad wrote 'look forward' on his sail. This had the desired effect and from then on he spent more time in the pizza zone and went on to become the GBR National Oppy Champion and 17th in the World!

The 'Pizza Zone'

Wind

upwind
'Pizza Zone'
Gusts, Lulls, Waves,
Shifts, etc

Use the 'Pizza Zone' to access information about what's going to happen next

TOP TIP
Learn to keep your head out of your boat! Concentrate on where you are going.

Gusts and Lulls — Changing Gear

Key to upwind speed is how you deal with gusts and lulls. Whenever you are sailing on a lake or, if the wind is offshore when sailing on the sea, you need to be aware of how to cope with gusty conditions.

You can usually see a gust coming on the water, a tell-tale darker patch of water is a sure sign of a gust, a lull looks greyer and lighter on the water.

Spot the gusts and lulls.

In a gust you will find that you can hike further out and harness more power. At the same time you need to be anticipating what is going to happen next so that you make a smooth transition into the next lull. You will be able to squeeze the main a little more in the gust and point a little higher in the lull. As the wind drops, you will need to ease your mainsheet and sit in.

Holding your Lane

One of the key skills to learn is, the ability to hold your lane when you are sailing upwind. If you can start well and hold your lane, you will be well on the way to becoming a successful Oppy sailor.

So what do you need to do to hold your lane? First of all you need to have a gap of about a boat length or more to leeward and be aware of what is going on around you. There will probably be gusts and lulls, so try to point higher in the gusts and don't forget to ease the main in the lulls. You need to be aware that there are lots of distractions from other boats, erratic waves and usually a bit of anxiety because you want to do well.

If the fleet starts to get headed, you will be able to see this happening because the boats to leeward suddenly seem way ahead. You need to point up to try and keep the gap closed, otherwise, you will fall into the lee bow of the boat to leeward. If you start to get lifted and seem to be going ahead of the boat to leeward, try to sail a little lower and faster to sail over the boat to leeward and to stop the boat to windward sailing over you!

Sailors holding their lanes upwind.

Even if you are struggling to hold your lane try not to tack off until you start to get headed or you can see a clear lane on the other tack or even 2 tacks ahead.

A Start

In a world class fleet, sailors can hold lanes for many minutes

B After 1 Minute

In our fleet B is lee bowed, C dropping back, E being sailed over

C After 2 Minutes

B out the back, C dropping back, E out the back

D After 3 Minutes

B out the back, C footed off a bit, E out the back. Think of the various options the boats have?

Other Boats

You can't avoid considering other boats when you are trying to sail fast because they can have a direct effect on your boat speed.

If you are sailing upwind close to other boats, they may be covering you giving you dirty wind. You might be lee bowing another boat, or the waves from your boat might be affecting another boat. The effect of being covered or lee bowed is so great that you need to avoid both. If you get trapped and you can't avoid them, you still need to be able to sail fast and hold your position.

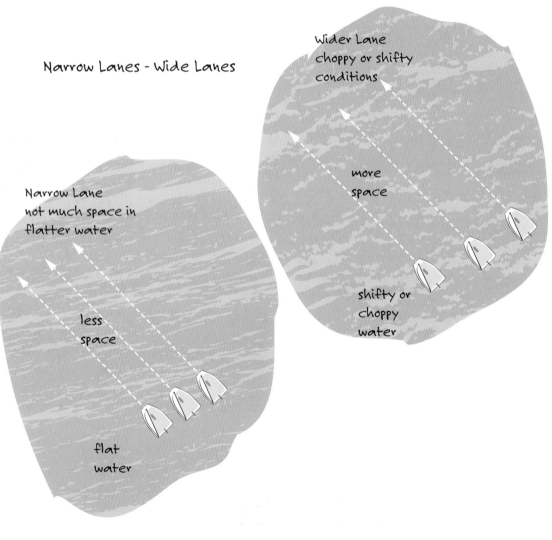

Narrow Lanes - Wide Lanes

Wider Lane
choppy or shifty
conditions

more
space

shifty or
choppy
water

Narrow Lane
not much space in
flatter water

less
space

flat
water

Being Covered or Lee Bowed

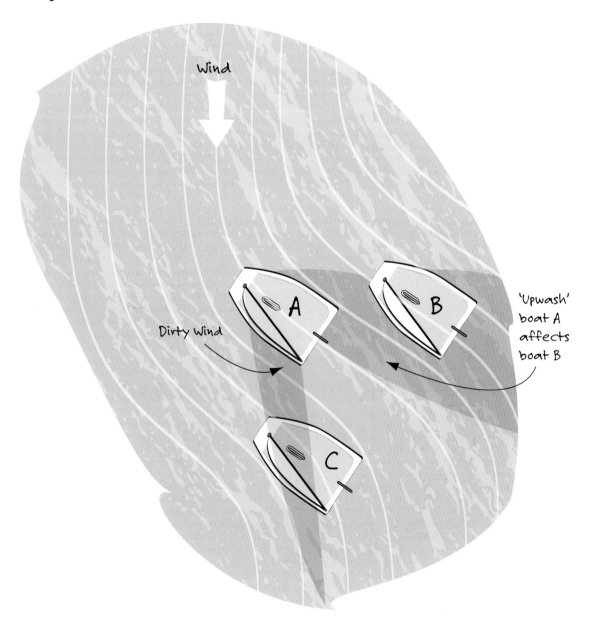

Boat A – is in clear wind
Boat B – is in headed wind caused by Boat A and is lee bowed
Boat C – is in Boat A's dirty wind and is covered

Bailing while Sailing

Bailing is a really important skill in an Oppy particularly upwind, and there's nothing worse than having water sloshing around in your Optimist. It's like a duck pond without the ducks and dead slow!

So you have to learn to keep your boat dry. Easy when the wind is light and progressively harder as it gets windy.

Water is heavy. 1 litre of water, which is about almost invisible in your boat, weighs about 1 kilogram, so if your are sailing around with about 5kg of water in your boat expect to go slow.

Let's have a look at the bailing technique:

• Pick up the bailer thumb towards you.

• Sit slightly further back in the boat and bail in a lull.

• If you have to – heel the boat to windward by hiking out or easing the main a little. The water will then come to the windward side of the boat.

• Lean in to do several positive quick bails and then carry on. Bigger sailors with longer arms find bailing easier than lighter sailors with shorter arms.

• If you are sailing on the sea wait for a flatter area to bail.

Really good hiking technique and good fitness leads to good bailing technique.

Upwind Technique

Now that we have explored what makes your boat go fast we'll take a look at sailing upwind in flat water and then in waves.

Flat Water

You need a smooth technique, no jerky movements which could upset the wind flow over your sail and remember to reduce your speed. Minimise the amount of rudder you use and use your body weight to steer the boat. In the gusts you can squeeze the main a little, point slightly higher and use more weight to keep the boat flat. As the gust starts to fade, ease the mainsheet slightly, slide your weight in and don't point quite so high.

To put it another way:

• When you are going fast you can squeeze the main a little and point higher.

• When you slow down in the lulls you need to ease the main a little and don't point quite so high – we might call this velocity looping.

Small Chop

Sailing upwind in chop, the technique is similar to flat water, but you also need to stop your bow ploughing into the waves. Make sure you are locked in your toestraps and use a rhythmic action leaning your shoulders towards the back of the boat to lift the bow over each small wave to smooth out the rocking action of your boat.

You can also take your mainsheet round your back leg which can help to hold you locked into your boat.

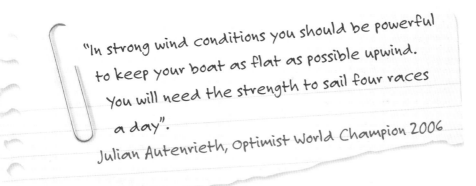

"In strong wind conditions you should be powerful to keep your boat as flat as possible upwind. You will need the strength to sail four races a day".
Julian Autenrieth, Optimist World Champion 2006

Waves — a bit of Science

Before looking at upwind sailing in bigger waves, we'll take a quick look at some of the science behind waves. Whether you are sailing on a lake or the sea, you will have to sail in waves which have a huge impact on your boat speed and the way you should be sailing your boat. We'll take a look at the mechanics and hydrology of waves before covering the specifics in the following sections.

What causes waves?

Waves are generally caused by the frictional effect of the wind on the water. You can demonstrate this by blowing across a bowl of water seeing that ripples form. Waves on lakes or the sea form in the same way and their size and shape depends on the distance the waves have travelled, the depth of the water and the strength of the wind.

Parts of a wave

The illustration below shows the various parts of a wave: height, crest, shoulders and trough.

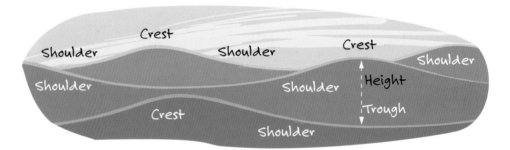

How fast is the wave travelling?

You don't really need to know how fast waves are travelling but it might surprise you to know that they move very quickly. A simple formula provides the answer.

Speed of a wave (knots) = 3 times the distance between two wave crests measured in seconds.

If the distance between wave crests is say 5 seconds then the wave is travelling at 15 knots (miles per hour).

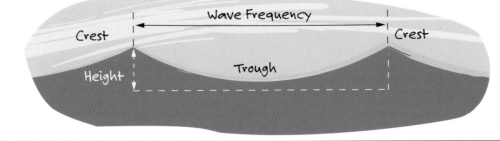

Water movement in the waves

The illustration shows just how the surface water moves in a wave. Basically the water moves in an orbital pattern and is travelling in different directions in different parts of the wave.

- Sailing upwind, it makes sense to spend as much time as possible in the troughs where the orbital pattern of water is going upwind. You need to spend as little time as possible on the crests when you are travelling uphill with the orbital flow of water against you.

- Downwind… it makes sense to spend as much time as possible surfing down the crests rather than wallowing in the troughs!

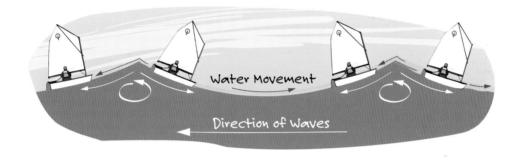

Water Movement

Direction of Waves

Upwind in Waves

- Sailing upwind in waves is a whole different game to sailing in flat water, you are trying to keep the boat sailing smoothly through the waves and trying to stop the boat pitching too much. You won't be able to point as high as on flat water and you have to sail slightly lower, or your boat will be very slow. Use a dynamic lean back body action to get you through the waves. In the flatter areas just sit angled slightly towards the back of the boat.

  - As you are sailing towards a wave, point up a little and lean back dynamically (towards the back of the boat) just before you get to the top of the wave. This will stop your bow slamming into the wave.

- On the top of the wave, sit upright and hike out if you need to.

- Keeping the boat flat bear away a little, lean slightly forward and ease the main slightly to get your speed up when going down the back of the wave.

- If you can't avoid a very steep or breaking wave, you might need to bear away around it.

- It's all about developing a rhythm in the ever changing waves.

- You can reduce water coming into your boat by heeling it to leeward, just as you go over the top of the wave. This makes your boat V shaped and water will tend to go to leeward of your boat.

You are bound to hit some waves or sets of waves that stop you in your tracks and you'll take some water onboard. If you are approaching a bigger wave, ease the mainsheet a little, to power up the sail and help you through the wave.

Sailing upwind in waves, bigger sailors sit slightly further back than normal.

Lean back to stop the boat hitting a wave.

Keep the boat sailing fast.

Check the next wave out.

Sailing fast between waves.

Occasionally you will get a wave wrong.
Don't worry. Keep your speed up.

Reaching

Reaching can sometimes seem to be something of a procession and most sailors just want to hold their positions. However, it's possible to make some great gains on a reach and particularly at the end of the reach, so let's look at the options.

• In sub-planing conditions, it is difficult to make big gains and a straightish route is often fastest in an Oppy unless there is tide (we will look at this later).

• Use the gusts and lulls, there will be big changes in boat speed and course sailed. Use the gusts to bear away and sail lower, then after the gust has passed, sail higher to meet the next gust, and you will be sailing a fast snaking path to the next mark.

• Don't, wait for your boat to slow down too much before heading up and, try to avoid using too much rudder.

• It's really important to make sure you adjust the mainsheet to keep the tell-tales flowing.

• If you are reaching in waves and a gust hits, try to wait until you can pick up a wave which will accelerate you. You'll find that the acceleration might backwind your sail, that's OK, just sheet in a little but, remember to ease the main as the boat slows down, then point back up in the next lull.

Perfectly balanced on the reach, AUS295 is bailing.

Fast Reaching - Planing

- Planing in an Oppy is great fun, your boat speed increases dramatically and you feel like you are flying over the waves.

- When your boat starts to sail fast on a reach, your boat overtakes your bow wave and starts to plane. Remember you usually have to sit back to get the boat planing and to stop the bow from burying. Trim your sail to keep the tell–tales flying. When your boat is planing, you need to sit slightly further forward to trim your boat properly.

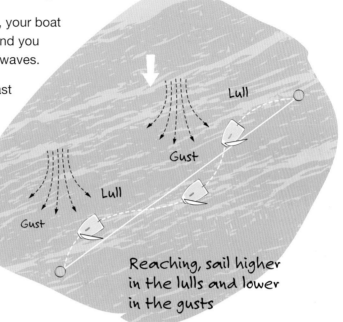

Reaching, sail higher in the lulls and lower in the gusts

- As you fall off the back of the wave, the boat will slow down dramatically and the apparent wind moves back. So dump the mainsheet back out, often called a lasso pump or negative pump - this isn't illegal and it resets the main. Then get ready for the next wave, have fun and if you are really smart you can link waves together.

- When sailing a close reach, you probably need to sail high because if you sail low, it is easy to fall into the dirty wind of the boats to windward. If it is a broader reach, you will often find a whole group sailing a big bow to windward to protect their wind. In this case, if you bear away and go low early there are some big gains to be made.

Running

The run can be like playing snakes and ladders with lots of gains and losses. Now we'll take a look at techniques for sailing on the run.

Light Winds

The aim is to keep the sail filling, so keep still in your boat and use very little rudder. Bring your daggerboard up to leave about 2cms in the water.

Top tip Mark your daggerboard to show ¼ up ½ up and ¾ up. You also need to ease your sprit tension to open the leech which is super quick.

Kiting an Oppy downwind.

- Let the mainsheet out so that the boom is just beyond 90 degrees which will hold the sail in position and heel the boat to windward reducing the wetted area of the hull, then raise the sail. We call this kiting.

- Kiting takes quite a lot of practice. In the early stages it is very easy to capsize to windward. Practise a lot and when the boat starts to heel over too much, just sheet in a little and put the daggerboard down a bit more to stabilise the boat.

- Turn your shoulders to point where you are going, with your front knee pointing towards the front of the boat.

- Look for gusts and position your boat to take advantage of them.

- Most sailors will hold the tiller extension at its base to make steering more accurate.

Medium Winds

The technique is similar to light winds, except that lightweights won't want to kite so much and, as waves start to appear, sit slightly further back in the boat. You will surf occasionally.

Downwind Wave Technique

When your boat starts to surge forwards on a wave, it's time to start surfing. The aim is to use the power in a wave to get your boat surfing (or planing quickly). It's great fun so you need a positive 'go for it' approach.

- Check back occasionally to position yourself for the best waves, usually the steepest.

- As a wave goes ahead and your stern lifts and bow drops, do one big pump and lean back hard to get your boat surfing. Sail as fast as you can, maybe on a very broad reach which will be faster than a run.

- Timing is everything, you need to practise a lot to get the feel of when to pump. There is usually an optimal point on each wave, a sweet spot, you'll just learn to know where it is.

- Keep the mainsheet sheeted in, then lean back and surf down the wave. Sit back upright again as you start to slow down and you get lower down the wave.

- You can steer your boat along the wave either by heading up – the upturn – or bearing away – the downturn. Remember because the wave is travelling forwards faster than you are, you will be sailing quickly downwind. Try to keep your boat on the steepest part of the wave.

- If it's a small wave, you can use a shorter pump, lean back and then upright again and move forward to keep your boat tracking down the wave.

- If it's a really big wave, try to avoid going dead down wind because you will probably nose dive.

- Remember, just as you fall off the back of the wave, the boat will really slow down and the apparent wind moves back. Use the lasso pump or negative pump by dumping the mainsheet out, sit forward and get ready for the next wave.

As you pick up a wave you're allowed one pump on the mainsheet. Note sailors leaning back.

N2L picks up the wave and surfs away from GBR.

Ready for the next wave.

The Rules only allow you to complete one pump on each wave. So your timing is really important to make each pump count.

Avoid the Death Roll

When you are sailing on a run and the leech of your sail goes forward beyond about 90 degrees you risk your boat becoming very unstable and rolling over to windward. To avoid this, don't let your sprit off too far when it's windy, and make sure that you have enough kicker to stop the boom rising and allowing the leech to open too much. If your boat starts to roll to windward, sheet in and lean in. If you are going down the run and you realise that you haven't got enough kicker, sheet in a little to prevent the death roll happening.

The death roll, the boat heels to windward and boat nearly capsizes.

The sailor regains control by sheeting in and leaning in.

THE SEARCH FOR SPEED

Strong Wind Running – Practise, Practise, Practise

Running is an exciting business especially in a strong breeze and you need to be really alert. So daggerboard about ¾ up, keep the sprit on and have loads of kicker. Let the boom out to about 80-85 degrees and sail the boat fairly flat sitting back to prevent the boat from nose diving. Keep your boat empty and avoid the bigger waves. Be very positive with the rudder and in the bigger gusts, sheet in a little and keep your boat pointing downwind. Steer positively, enjoy yourself and sing a song or hum a favourite piece of music.

In total control, sailing downwind on a rough day.

Short steep choppy waves in an offshore wind off Sardinia.

Optimist tuning guide

Use this guide as basic settings and when you become more experienced adjust them to suit your sailing style, the sail you use and your height and weight.

Wind Strength	Upwind Light Force 1-2	Upwind Medium Force 2-4	Upwind Strong Force 4-6+	Reach Light Force 1-2	
Mast Rake	Basic setting 282-284cms or 111-112 inches measured without kicker from the top of the mast to top of rear gunwale.				
Mast Ties	Top and bottom eased to 6-7mm middle 2-3mm off touching mast or, if lazy, all ties about 5mm off mast.	All ties 4-5mm off mast – personal choice.	All ties 3-4mm off mast for heavier sailors top and bottom ties just off mast middle ties 4-5mm off mast.		
Boom Ties	5mm at the ends and up to 7-8mm in the middle.				
Kicker	Slack.	Just loose upwind and getting tighter.	Tight becoming very tight.	Slack.	
Outhaul	Slightly tighter than smooth foot shape.	Smooth foot shape.	Firm, but not too tight because you still need power in bottom of sail.		
Luffing	Slack, to keep draft back allowing pointing.	Slack to medium as wind increases, to pull draft forward. If choppy firmer, to give more power but less pointing.	Tighter, to pull draft forward and open leech.		
Sprit	Creases at throat.	Throat creases just disappear.	Tight, lightweights ease sprit to show crease at throat depowering the sail. When very windy all have an eased sprit.		

Reach Medium Force 2-4	Reach Strong Force 4-6+	Run Light Force 1-2	Run Medium Force 2-4	Run Strong Force 4-6+
Radial sails might need the mast slightly further forward than cross cut sails.				
Mast sail ties twice round mast, using 1.5-2mm pre stretched cord. Top mast, diagonal, tack and clew ties 3mm cord around mast and boom 2-3 times.				
Make sure ties don't stretch.				
As upwind. Lightweights tight.	Very tight.	Slack.	As upwind. Lightweights tight.	Very tight or you won't get downwind.
All sails have different foot lengths so you need to adjust your sail accordingly. Mark your settings on your boom.				
All sails are designed slightly differently. Some like a generally softer luff tension and others firmer tension. Check your sail tuning guide. Set luff tension using twists on the boom and the pin stop on mast. The diagonal tie setting is really, really important and make sure you replace the diagonal if it starts to wear.				
In light to medium winds as you get more experienced, learn to ease your sprit downwind and put it on again after you have rounded the leeward mark.				

Optimist tuning guide

Wind Strength	Upwind Light Force 1-2	Upwind Medium Force 2-4	Upwind Strong Force 4-6+	Reach Light Force 1-2
Mainsheet and Boom Span	2:1 or 3:1 Maybe use lightweight 6mm sheet.	3:1 purchase 7-8mm non absorbent mainsheet.	3:1 purchase 7- 8mm non-absorbent mainsheet.	←
Sheeting	Boom just outside corner of boat. Keep leech tell-tales flowing.	Sheeted into corner, ease in lulls. Keep leech tell-tales flowing.	Sheeted into corner, ease in gusts.	Keep tell-tales flowing.
Daggerboard (Mark positions on board)	Down.	Down. Light-weights can raise the board a little if overpowered.	Up to 100mm up, even for heavier sailors, if struggling to hold boat upright.	½ way up.
Light Weight Sailing Position	Progressively kneel by mainsheet block, sit on thwart then perch on side, bottom in, shoulders out.	Sit on side, bottom in, shoulders out. Shoulders slightly back to lift bow over chop.	Hike heaps, dynamic body movement, shoulders to back of boat to get over each wave.	Sit on thwart, then perch on side.
Heavy Weight Sailing Position	Kneel between mainsheet or sit on thwart. Bottom in, shoulders out.	Perch on side, bottom in, shoulders out. Start shoulders back to lift bow over chop.	Hike dynamically, weight back to get through waves.	Sit on thwart, then perch on side.
Steering	Smooth, use body weight to steer. Little use of rudder.	Smooth, still using body weight to steer. Gradually use rudder a little to get through chop.	Use more rudder to sail through chop and waves.	Smooth, use body to steer.

Reach Medium Force 2-4	Reach Strong Force 4-6+	Run Light Force 1-2	Run Medium Force 2-4	Run Strong Force 4-6+
Generally the boom span wants to be tight, set the depth to about 80mm. Use a mainsheet strop of up to 225mm or 11 inches between the bottom and top mainsheet blocks to reduce the amount of mainsheet you use and reduce windage. Bigger sailors can move the mainsheet position on the boom strop forward to nearly above the thwart to give more room to tack without sinking the back of the boat.				
Keep tell-tales flowing.	Keep tell-tales flowing.	Boom out to 90/95 degrees.	Boom out to 90 degrees.	Boom out to about 80 degrees.
½ way up.	¾ way up.	Tip just showing or pulled right up.	¾ way up.	¾ way up.
Hike, shoulders back slightly.	Hike heaps, slide forward to trim boat when planing.	Kite.	Kiteless.	Keep boat fairly flat.
Hike shoulders back slightly.	Hike heaps, slide forward to trim boat when planing.	Almost fully kited.	Fully kited.	Slightly kited/ keep boat flat when windy.
Smooth – using body to steer. Bear away in gusts, head up in lulls.	Use a little more rudder, bear away in gusts, head up in lulls.	Smooth, use body to steer.	Smooth, use body to steer.	Use more rudder to sail through chop and catch waves. Have fun.

Mark rounding is another important skill which can lead to significant gains and losses, so we'll take a look at some key aspects of mark roundings.

Windward Mark Approach

Your approach to the windward mark affects your options on the rounding.

• If you are having to pinch (sail above close hauled) to get round the mark because you misjudged the approach.

• The tide is pushing you down onto the mark.

• Someone has just tacked right on top of you.

You need to keep your wits about you to get out of trouble. If you are approaching with some space slightly above the layline or the tide is taking you up the course you will have a much easier rounding.

If you are bearing away around the windward mark, the classic approach would be to ease the main, heel the boat slightly to windward and pull the daggerboard up. However, if you have slightly overstood the windward marks, you can ease the mainsheet earlier and it will be possible to raise the daggerboard just before you round the mark.

A will tack and
  round ahead

B needs to duck
  some boats and
  find a lane

C won't get round -
  get out of
  there early

D will get round
  second

E has sailed
  further but will
  be near the front
  rounding

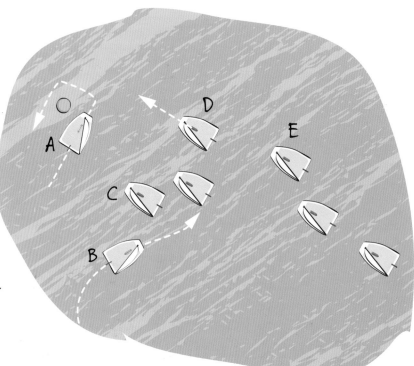

Rounding onto a Reach

As the breeze increases mark rounding becomes more dynamic and as you bear away you will need to hike hard. Move back in the boat to prevent the bow from nose diving and don't forget to make sure you have bailed before you get to the mark.

Windward mark approach, note the boats coming in on the port which need to find a gap.

If you are coming in on port and you are tacking around the mark, give yourself plenty of room and be prepared to hike hard to make the boat bear away around the mark after you have tacked. If really windy, a port tack approach close to the mark isn't a good idea. So instead come in well below the port layline, get onto starboard quite a few boat lengths before the mark, and then bear away.

Bearing away onto a reach tends to be easier than onto a run. If you haven't managed to get the daggerboard up before you round, get the boat going, ease the main, do a snappy daggerboard up and carry on.

1) Get ready to ease the mainsheet.

2) Ease the mainsheet.

3) Steer onto a reach.

4) Daggerboard up.

Rounding onto a Run

Bearing away onto a run is usually straightforward, but what you need to think about is the dirty wind from the boats behind you. OK, if you are well ahead, you can bear away and aim for the mark or even gybe, but if you are in the pack and you bear away straight onto a run you could be blanketed by the boat behind. So make a slightly wider turn to keep your air clear.

When it gets really windy, give the windward mark a wider rounding and make a wider turn. This makes sure you control the transition from beating to running. The key skill is to keep sailing as fast as possible and your boat will pop up onto the plane. Don't forget to try to make sure that your boat has been bailed dry before you round the mark.

Sprit on the Run

There is no doubt that easing your sprit in light to medium winds and opening up the leech on the run is super quick. Simply lean forward and ease the sprit off a little while steering in a straight line. Bigger sailors will be able to ease the sprit more easily than smaller sailors, who might find it just too hard to ease the sprit at all!

Easing the sprit.

Sailing on a run in Uruguay.

Leeward Mark Roundings

Leeward mark roundings are really important, they set you up for the next windward leg and also affect your tactics and strategy. So let's look at the options.

Light to Medium Winds

The aim here is to enter **wide** and exit **tight** in a smooth action without using too much rudder. In light to medium winds you can really heel your boat to leeward and sheet in. This spins the boat very nicely.

Leeward mark rounding

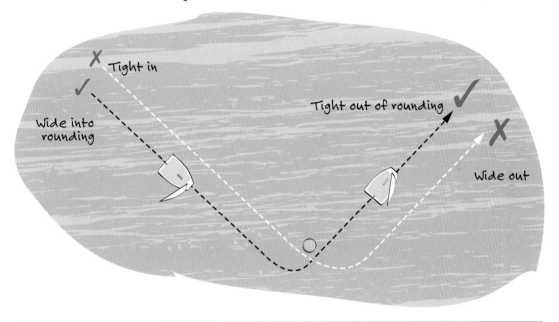

Tight in

Tight out of rounding

Wide into rounding

Wide out

Strong Winds

Keep the boat flat and turn the boat smoothly, hiking and sheeting in from a hiking position as you head up. The technique is to turn the boat and sheet in.

Traffic

Unless you are in the leading group, you are often in traffic rounding a mark. Be careful rounding – if the boat ahead of you slows down, it might force you to leeward (outside) – which would be a disaster. Look ahead and see what's going on. It is better to slow down a little to get your bow up above the transom of the boat ahead, to hold your height. You will then be able to carry on for some time and make your own decision about when to tack.

5412 makes a perfect rounding getting inside 5287.

Adjust your Sprit

If you have eased your sprit to sail fast downwind, you now have the tricky problem of putting the sprit back on to sail back upwind.

- Lean forward and put the sprit on before you round or, wait until after you have rounded. When you put your sprit back on depends upon where you are in the pack. Ideally, round the mark.
- Hold your position and height until you are well clear of the mark, then use the following technique:

  1 Make sure you are close hauled, ease the mainsheet, keeping the rudder straight.

  2 Sit forward, then stand up.

  3 Let go of the tiller extension, step forward (with your front foot over the windward side of the thwart).

  4 Bend at the knees, you are now in a sort of surfer dude position.

  5 Grab the sprit handle and in one smooth movement, give it a good smooth jab downwards.

  6 Then step back, grab the tiller extension, sit down, sheet in and carry on.

This seems like a lot to do, (it is) but you should, with practice, be able to do it in about 2 seconds. If your boat bears away you may have put your front foot too far to windward, so next time put your front foot closer to the centre line.

Round the leeward mark.

Ease the mainsheet and stand up.

Step forward and put your sprit on.

Putting the sprit on.

Sit down and sheet in.

There's a message in the clouds

Watch out for the effect of features

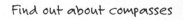

Find out about compasses

'Never give up and
never limit your options -
use the elements to
your advantage'

Nick Thompson
Optimist European Champion
Laser Youth World Champion
Laser sailor

Before you go charging around the race track it is useful to understand what effect the wind, weather, waves, tide and geographical features will have on your boat. The next few chapters are designed to give lots of information to help you with the decisions you have to make.

What causes Wind?

Worldwide weather systems are caused by the sun's warming effect on the earth, and the type of land or sea that the sun is heating up. What happens is, that the sun heats up the land which heats the air mass above it and the air rises, just like steam rises from a kettle.

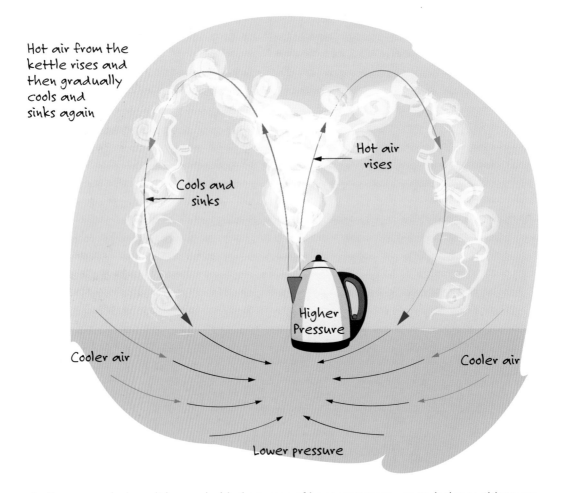

Hot air from the kettle rises and then gradually cools and sinks again

Hot air rises

Cools and sinks

Higher Pressure

Cooler air

Cooler air

Lower pressure

As the warm air rises, it leaves behind an area of lower pressure, so to balance things up some more air moves in to take its place. The air that has risen gets blown to another area by the strong upper winds and eventually starts to sink again as it cools.

This process causes wind. The important thing to remember is that wind always goes from higher to lower pressure. Just how strong the wind will be, depends upon the difference in pressure between low and high pressure, what we call the pressure gradient.

Weather people use big computers to work out what will happen with the wind and weather and they produce weather maps called synoptic charts.

• Weather charts are great because they show the pressure in lines called isobars.

• Isobars show lines of equal pressure.

• The gap between each isobar can be measured to give a good idea of wind strength and direction.

• Charts also show areas of low pressure and areas of high pressure. The wind nearly always flows along the isobars. If it is an area of low pressure the wind is angled slightly in towards the centre of the low. If it is high pressure, the wind is angled slightly towards the outside of the high. Wind blowing along the isobars is called gradient wind.

One other thing you might have heard of is the Coriolis Effect. The earth spins to the right and as a result in the Northern Hemisphere the wind is deflected to the right and the left in the Southern Hemisphere.

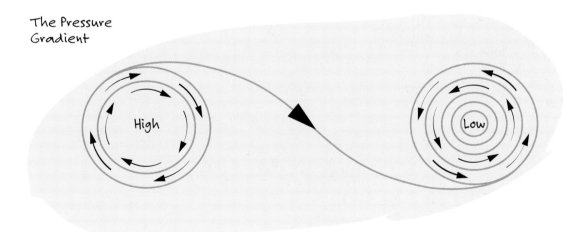

The Pressure Gradient

High

Low

Wind flows from high to low pressure

Weather

There are two types of weather systems that you need to be aware of:

• Low pressure systems or depressions

• High pressure systems or anticyclones.

Low Pressure Systems

Lows look like a dartboard of isobars. The wind circulates anticlockwise and different parts of the low are at different temperatures and have more or less moisture. Where warm and colder air meet is called a front, there are two main types of front:

• Warm front

• Cold front

Both bring rain and after they pass over you the wind will veer to the right. Occasionally these two fronts catch up with each other and result in an occluded front. Lows generally bring unsettled weather and wind with them.

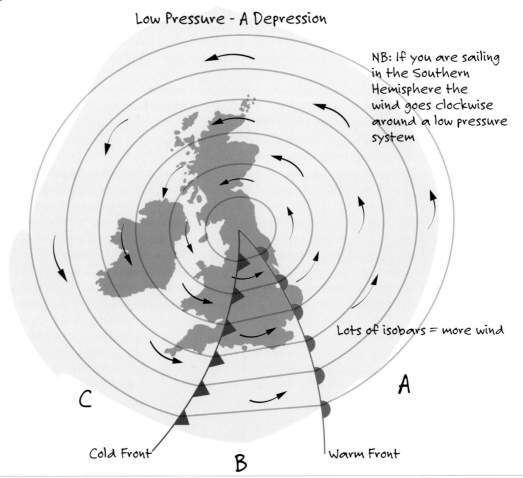

Low Pressure - A Depression

NB: If you are sailing in the Southern Hemisphere the wind goes clockwise around a low pressure system

Lots of isobars = more wind

A

C

Cold Front

B

Warm Front

High Pressure

A high pressure system has fewer isobars and generally settled weather. In the summer, high pressure usually means great settled sunny weather with lighter winds. You might also get some thermal activity and sea breezes may develop.

High Pressure

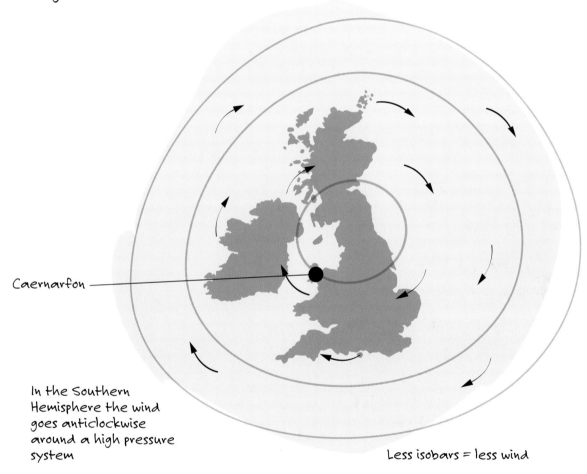

Caernarfon

In the Southern Hemisphere the wind goes anticlockwise around a high pressure system

Less isobars = less wind

Anyway enough of all that science stuff!

Wind Strength

Some time ago in 1805 before Oppys were invented, Admiral Beaufort developed a wind scale which after a while the Royal Navy adopted because they were fed up that the sails were blowing off their sailing ships! There were no hi-tech sail makers to repair the sails so they decided to produce a wind scale so that the sailors knew which sail to use and when. The scale is still in use today to estimate wind strength.

The wind is measured in knots and one knot is just over 1 land mile per hour (or 1852 metres per hour).

The Beaufort Scale for Oppy Sailors

Wind force	Strength	Sea state and sailing conditions
1	1-3 knots	Ripples - drifting conditions. Sailors hope for more wind.
2	4-6 knots	Small wavelets - still sitting in. Small sailors sit on the side
3	7-10 knots	Occasional white horses (wave crests). Big sailors get to sit on the side.
4	11-16 knots	Frequent white horses. Sitting out having fun, lightweights hiking hard. Bailing of course!
5	17-21 knots	Moderate waves, pretty windy, bigger waves. Big sailors having fun, small sailors hiking very hard and bailing a lot!
6	22-27 knots	Large waves at sea. Very gusty on a lake. Difficult sailing conditions and only the very experienced will cope.
7	28-34 knots	Optimists blow off trolleys. Parents start jumping up and down, everyone goes home.

There's no point in looking at force 8 and 9 because we would be too busy stopping ourselves from being blown away in the dinghy park!

WIND & WEATHER

Weather Information

Loads of weather information is available, from television, radio, newspapers and the internet. Internet weather reports are really good, simply load your favourite locations and you can check them out in the days leading up to an event and build up a picture of the weather. A word of warning - weather forecasters are great people and they use big computers to crunch the numbers to come up with forecasts, but it's not possible for them to get it right all of the time and local effects can significantly affect the wind and weather. A local effect is caused by the effect of the land, hills, estuaries etc.

Onshore Winds — Lee Shore

Onshore winds tend to be steady, because they come from out at sea. When you are standing on the shore, they often feel stronger than they actually are and the waves are always bigger on a lee shore. Often, there is a temptation to rig for windy conditions and when you get afloat it's less windy than you thought.

Returning to the beach in an onshore wind.

Onshore wind.

Offshore Winds - Weather Shore

Offshore winds can be very gusty because the wind has crossed the land before going out to sea or onto a lake. The waves are often small because they are only just forming but will be bigger further offshore. The wind often feels lighter on shore than it is when you get afloat.

Gusty conditions close to the windward or weather shore, spot the gusts.

Thermal Winds – Sea Breezes

In the summer months on the coast when the sun is shining, a sea breeze often develops. The sea breeze is a micro high - low pressure system.

As the sea breeze sets, in the wind usually goes further right so on a sea breeze day it often pays to protect the right hand side of the course, (the left in the Southern Hemisphere).

The sun heats the land and by mid morning the air above starts to rise causing low pressure close to the ground and sheep-like Cumulus clouds form. Cool air from the sea moves in to balance the pressure and by mid afternoon it's possible to have a good Force 4 blowing. (See The Beaufort Scale, page 126.) The wind will generally track right during the afternoon and as the sun starts to get lower in the sky, the sea breeze will start to die away. In the Southern Hemisphere the wind will track left as the sea breeze develops.

The Sea Breeze

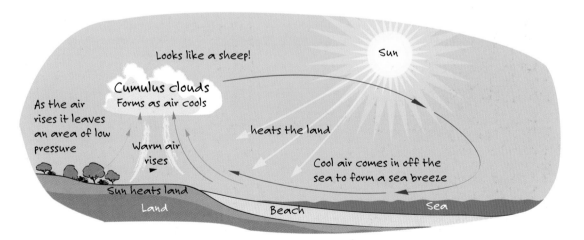

Looks like a sheep!

Sun

Cumulus clouds Forms as air cools

As the air rises it leaves an area of low pressure

heats the land

Warm air rises

Cool air comes in off the sea to form a sea breeze

Sun heats land

Land   Beach   Sea

Clouds

Clouds do have an effect on sailing, particularly the lower clouds like Cumulus clouds. The reason Cumulus clouds affect us is that, to form in the first place, air close to the ground is warmed by the sun (due to thermal activity), the air rises and as it gets colder, the moisture in the air condenses and puffy cumulus clouds form.

If you sail under one of these clouds, the wind is generally much lighter due to the air being sucked up into the cloud. You need to avoid sailing under these white based clouds unless you want to go slow. You will be better off looking for the blue sky areas, where there will be more wind.

White Based Cloud

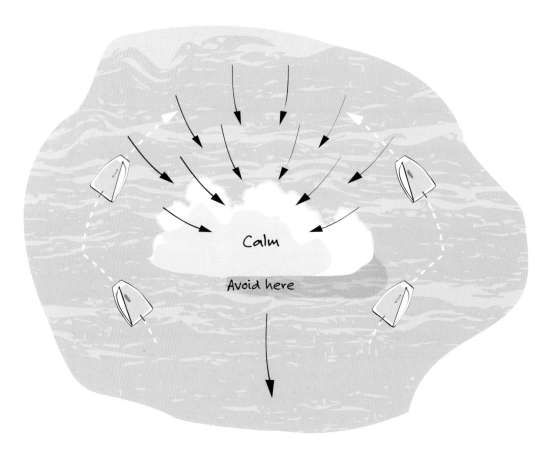

If you see a Cumulus cloud with a dark base or if it's raining out of it, that is a sure sign of stronger cooler air blowing out from the base of the cloud. You can sail over towards it and make some gains.

Dark Based or Raining Cloud

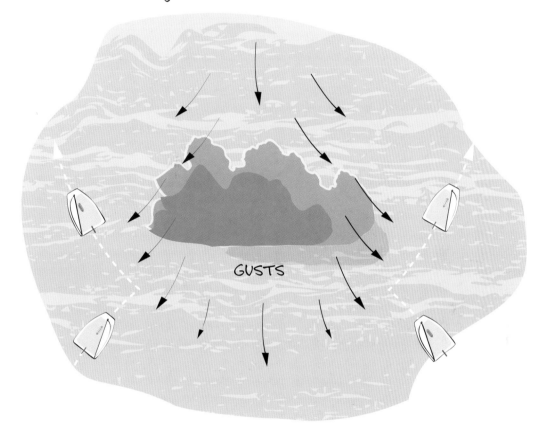

GUSTS

A Shifty Business

Now that you know what causes wind, you need to work out how to use the wind when you are sailing. The wind is rarely steady and that means there is usually one tack, called the lifted tack, when sailing upwind. Remember, that the lifted tack is the one that leads you more towards the windward mark. Be aware that you don't always need to be on a lift to be making a gain – we will look at this later.

To start off, let's look at a simple principle – always know if you're being lifted or headed. It's a very important skill and the basis for most of your decision making.

So how do we know? Here's a few ideas…

Relative Position

The simple way to tell if you are lifted or headed is the relative position of your boat to other boats.

- If the boat to leeward appears to be pulling ahead; you are being headed.

- If you appear to be pulling ahead of the boat to leeward; you are being lifted. Unless of course you are sailing super quick!

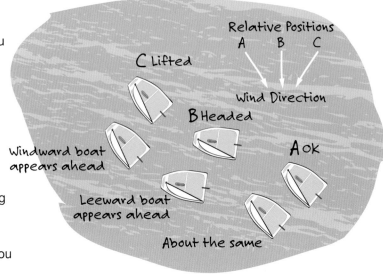

Lifted or Headed Relative Positions

Relative Positions
A   B   C

C Lifted

Wind Direction

B Headed

A ok

Windward boat appears ahead

Leeward boat appears ahead

About the same

Use the Shore

Another simple way to tell what's happening while you are sailing upwind is to look at the shore. If you are pointing at something like a tree, then suddenly or gradually if you can't point that high anymore you have been headed. If you can point higher than the tree you have been lifted - easy really, isn't it! Unless you are sailing in tidal areas, when you will need to know which way the tide is going.

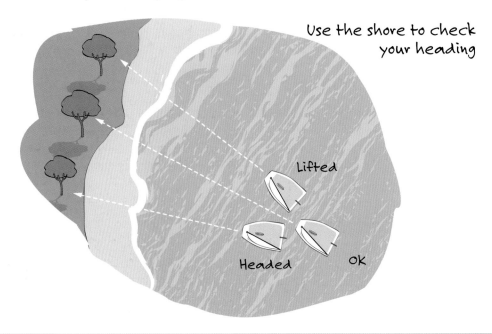

Use the shore to check your heading

Lifted

Headed   OK

Windward Mark

You can use the windward mark as a reference point, as a rule of thumb you need to be on the tack taking you closest to the windward mark, not the one taking you furthest from it.

Use your Compass

If you are using a compass, the numbers will show if you have been headed or lifted. If there are only a few boats around you or you are sailing out towards the sea with no land features, a compass can help you work out if you have been lifted or headed.

Random Chaotic Shifts

When you are sailing on a lake or in an offshore wind, it can be very shifty with no particular pattern and lots of gusts and lulls. In this situation you need to make sure you are on the lifted tack, that is the tack taking you closest to the windward mark unless you have a reason not to!

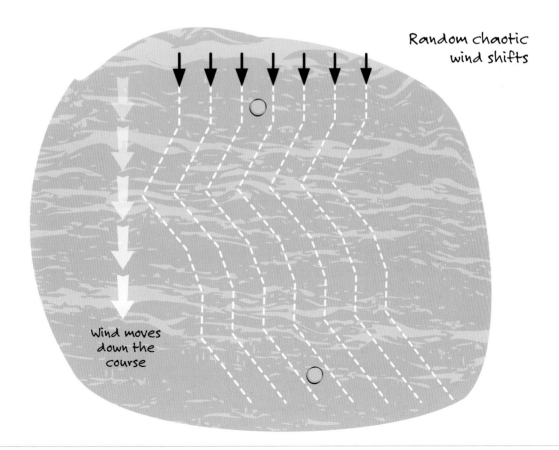

Random chaotic wind shifts

Wind moves down the course

Gusts and Lulls

- Gusts of wind come from higher up in the sky and show up as dark patches on the water. They tend to be a bit colder and often, but not always, come from slightly further right.

- Lulls in the wind show up as lighter patches, and often feel warmer than a gust. They generally come from slightly further left.

This would suggest to use starboard tack in the gusts and port tack in the lulls, except that it's not always quite that simple!

Spot the gusts and lulls.

Take a look at the diagram and you will see that a gust can often come at you like a spread out hand. Depending upon where the gust hits, you could be lifted, about the same, or headed. The skill is to link these gusts together as you sail upwind.

Gusts and Lulls

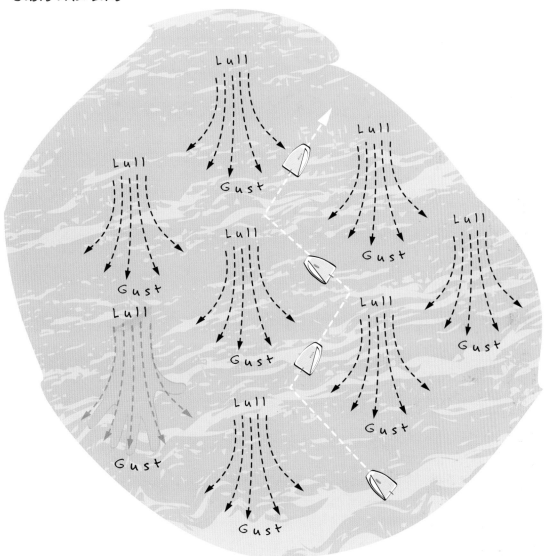

Gusts hit the water and spread out downwind (like spreading out the fingers on your hand). Use the edges of the gusts to make your way upwind by linking the gusts together.

Velocity Header

Imagine that you are sailing along upwind, and then a gust comes. The increased wind strength will enable you to point higher because your sail and foils generate more lift. This is a velocity lift. As the gust goes you won't be able to point quite so high. Don't mistake this for a header, it is simply a velocity header.

Wait for a real header!

Persistent Shift

This sort of shift should be easy to recognise and if you have done your homework, you might have been expecting the wind to shift one way during the day.

On a sea breeze day, the wind might be going to the right all day. If a weather system is coming you might be expecting a front to pass and the wind to veer to the right. In some complex weather patterns the wind might back to the left. Either way what matters is that you know which way the wind is going to shift.

Sail towards the next shift or new wind

Wind moves right

Old Wind

New Wind

Be careful how far you go into the header or you could overstand the windward mark

Take header into shift first

To take advantage of a persistent shift you have to first recognise that there is one. To make a gain you need to sail into the persistent shift on the headed tack, (yes, the headed tack), to get inside the rest of the fleet. Then tack and as the wind gradually frees you, you will lift up inside the fleet. It's a bit like getting onto the inside of a running track because you sail a shorter distance.

All this is great if it is a slow persistent shift, but if it is shifting fast, you might end up over standing the windward mark. So be careful, don't be greedy, don't go too far inside the shift too early.

The boats on the left are lifting inside boats on the right. Note 6999 on starboard going left to get inside the shift.

These sailors are heading towards the cliffs to take advantage of the stronger wind nearer the cliffs.

Oscillations

Oscillating breezes can be a bit of a challenge. First of all you need to be able to recognise that the wind is oscillating. Then what should you do about it?

A true oscillating breeze will swing left and right about the same amount from a particular direction. But this does not happen very often. What usually happens, is that the oscillation wanders around a bit.

Sometimes an oscillation might be very short, say every few minutes and sometimes it could be over a much longer time period; for example 30 minutes and may feel more like a persistent shift.

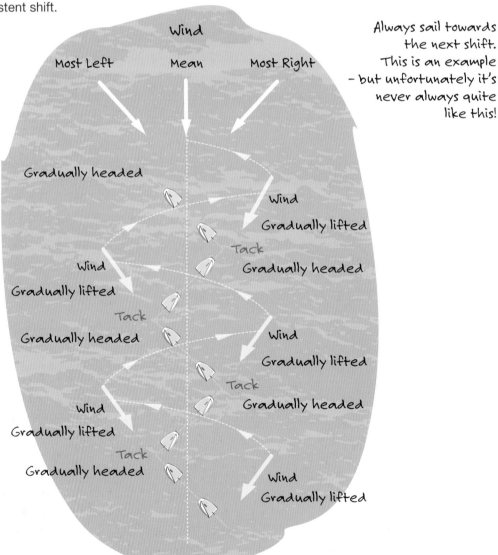

Wind

Most Left   Mean   Most Right

Always sail towards the next shift. This is an example – but unfortunately it's never always quite like this!

Gradually headed

Wind
Gradually lifted

Tack
Gradually headed

Wind
Gradually lifted

Tack
Gradually headed

Wind
Gradually lifted
Gradually headed

Tack

Wind
Gradually lifted

Tack
Gradually headed

Wind
Gradually lifted

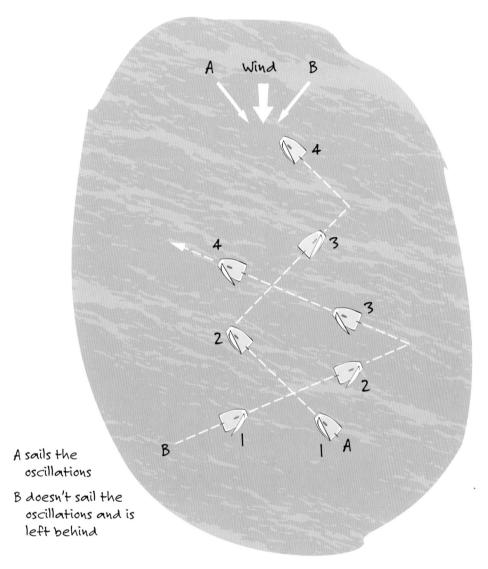

A sails the oscillations

B doesn't sail the oscillations and is left behind

When the wind is oscillating you don't tack as soon as you get headed. You tack after you have passed the mean or average wind direction and dug into the header a bit. How far past the mean you go before you tack, depends upon how long the oscillation is and how much of a risk you want to take. If the oscillation is short in time and angle, tack soon. If the oscillation is long and slow, you need to sail further into the shift before tacking. How far - well that's an interesting question. When to tack is just like the persistent shift because long slow oscillations are just like mini persistent shifts. If they are fast and a big angle, tack earlier and if they are slow tack later - it all comes down to experience and practice. When the wind starts going back the other way, you will be progressively headed back to the mean and you'll need to dig into the header before you tack.

Convergence and Divergence

Have you ever heard of land on the left, go left? Let's take a look at what it means.

Because of the frictional effects of the wind on the land the wind over the land is slowed and backs to the left. This backing effect can be considerable, less on flat land and more for trees and hills. The sea generally has less of a frictional effect so the wind is less backed.

- If the land is on the left, the wind is backed over the land. The backed wind off the shore converges with the wind on the sea, creating a stronger wind closer to the shore.

- If the land is on the right, the wind again backs. The wind on the water and the wind on the land are diverging and there is less wind.

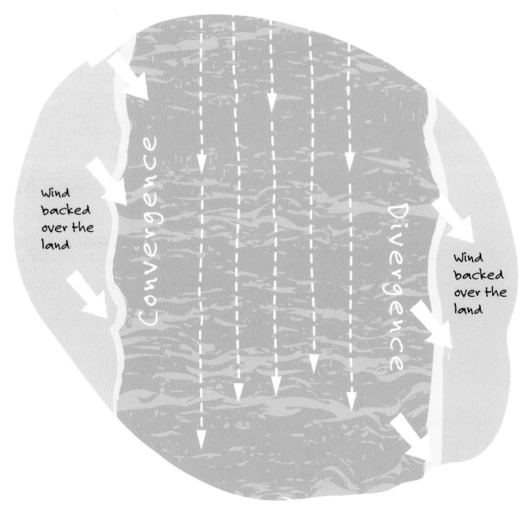

Wind backed over the land

Convergence

Divergence

Wind backed over the land

In theory, land on the left, go left, but it's not always that simple!

Windward Shore

If the wind is coming off the windward shore there will usually be a wind bend close to the shore. Looking upwind, the wind will usually veer to the right as the wind comes off the shore creating a wind bend. Going left into the bend and then lifting out of it, can result in good gains.

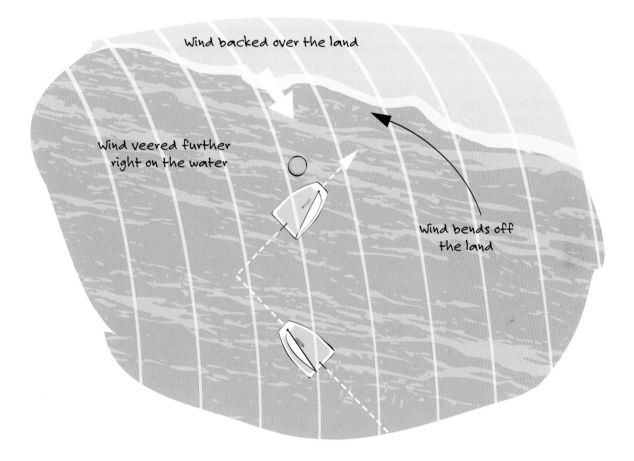

Bend near the windward shore

The Last Shift

When you get really experienced, the last shift into the windward mark can be very interesting and needs to be treated as a permanent shift. You dig into the headed tack, tacking and then lift inside to the mark. Don't overdo it or you might just overstand the windward mark.

Last Shift into the
Windward Mark

Wind shifts left

Take header
on Starboard
then lift higher
on Port

Even when you are sailing upwind in waves you need to know what the wind is doing.

Geographical features have a huge local effect on the wind. When you're walking around town on a blustery day the wind comes from all sorts of directions. That's because the wind is forced to bend in all sorts of directions. So let's take a look at these various features and see how they affect the wind.

Land and Water

When the wind blows over the land it is affected by the shape of the land and what is growing on it. All land slows down the wind by friction and as it slows down it is generally backed or moves left. More friction equals more backed left. If the land is made up of low fields then the wind will back less, but more if there are trees about. Valleys and mountains usually cause the wind to be forced in a number of different directions.

There is usually less friction over water, so the wind on water comes from closer to the gradient wind direction - that's the one more in line with the isobars.

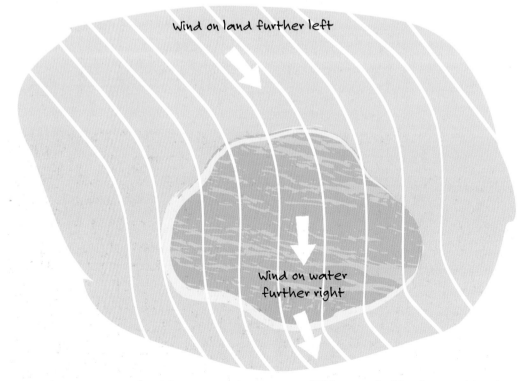

Wind on land further left

Wind on water further right

Effect of Friction on the Land

Hills, Valleys and Headlands

- So as we have seen if there are hills, valleys and headlands then the wind will be radically changed from the forecast direction.

- The wind is forced around and over hills and it will funnel down valleys.

- If a headland pushes out into the race course you can be sure that it will have a big effect on the wind causing what is known as a wind bend.

- The effect of a wind bend is simple. It is just like a running track, the further inside the bend you are, the shorter the distance to sail. Remember, don't go into the bend too much, because you might overstand the windward mark.

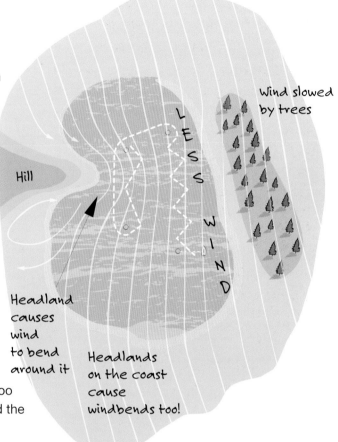

Wind slowed by trees

Hill

LESS WIND

Headland causes wind to bend around it

Headlands on the coast cause windbends too!

The small headland at A causes a windbend.

Obstacles in the Wind

When you are on the start line looking upwind, start thinking about the effect that the features will have on the wind. You will be able to think of a lot of barriers: trees, hills, valleys, a sailing club and even a group of boats on a start line. Just look at a feature and think about how the wind will be deflected around or over it causing bends, shifts or more or less wind.

These Optimists create a barrier to the wind.

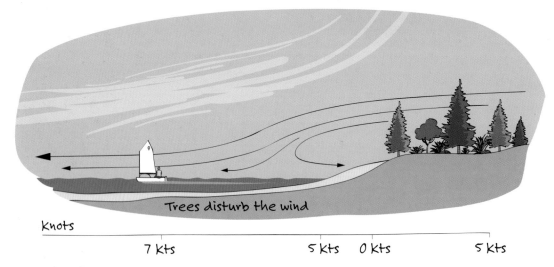

Trees disturb the wind

Knots

| | 7 kts | | 5 kts | 0 kts | | 5 kts |

Here is an example of how a fleet acts as a barrier to the wind.

Note that the Optimist startline presents a barrier to the wind. Get on the front row.

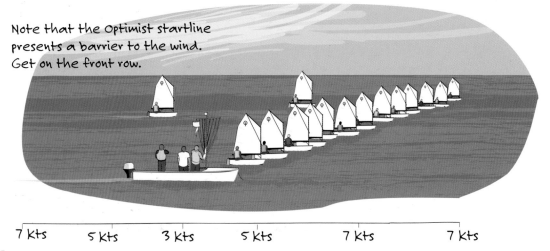

| 7 kts | 5 kts | 3 kts | 5 kts | 7 kts | 7 kts |

Lake Sailing

If you are sailing on a lake, you really need to get used to the way the land around the lake affects the wind. Write yourself notes for different wind directions to help build up a picture of what happens in different wind directions and on different lakes. A lot of the information on shifts we have looked at applies to sailing on lakes. The wind will tend to be steadier on large lakes with low surrounding land, but a lake surrounded by large hills can cause very unstable winds. Small lakes might only have random chaotic shifts, gust and lulls, which are great practice for sea sailors.

Lots of sailing takes place on coastal waters, either on the open sea or in bays and estuaries, so we'd better take a look at how the tide can affect sailing.

Gravity

Here is some useful information you need to know about sailing on tidal waters.

The Sun and the Moon have a gravitational pull effect upon the earth, this pull causes tides. There are usually two high and two low waters each day and the gravitational pull also causes tidal streams which move back and forth around the coastline.

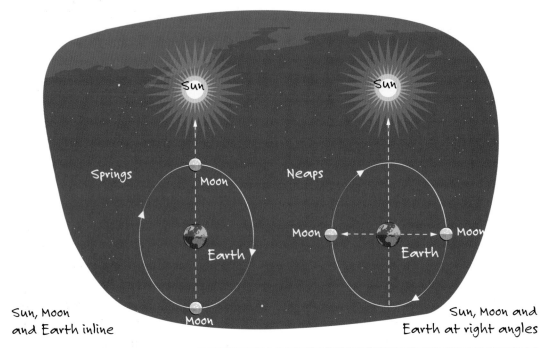

Sun, Moon and Earth inline

Sun, Moon and Earth at right angles

Springs and Neaps

It takes about 28 days for the Earth to rotate around the Moon and during that time we have Spring and Neap tides. Every month on average we get: a week of springs, and then, a week of neaps, then a week of springs, then a week of neaps and so on.

Springs

Occur about every 14 days when the Earth, Moon and Sun are in line (see the illustration above). When this happens we get higher – high waters and lower – low waters.

Neaps

Occur about seven days after springs when the Sun, Moon and Earth are at right angles. We now get lower - high waters and higher - low waters.

High and Low Water

Each day it takes about 6 hours to get from low water to high water and 6 hours to get back to low water again, so we have 2 high waters and 2 low waters every day. As an example:

- If high water was at midnight, low water would be at 6am.
- High water at 12 noon, low water at 6pm. Each day high water is just under an hour later than the day before, so if high water was 12 noon today, it will be just before 13.00 tomorrow.

Tide Times

To find out what time high or low water is, you can check an almanac, a club website, or local tide tables. The tidal information needs to be local to where you are sailing because the times of high and low water are different in different places on the same day. Be warned, it's not an exact science and if you are sailing up an estuary or a creek, tide times will again be different.

When out sailing, high and low water times are only really important if you don't want a long walk pulling your boat up or down the beach!

Tidal Streams

The gravitational pull also causes tidal streams which move back and forth around the coastline. From a racing sailor's point of view, knowing what the tidal stream is doing is essential. Tidal streams are measured in knots and a knot is about 1.1 land miles per hour. Tidal streams vary in strength from place to place and whether it is springs or neaps. On spring tides the tidal stream runs stronger and on neaps the stream is about 2/3rds of the spring rate.

Tidal streams are referred to as the flood or the ebb streams and an important point is that slack water, when the tidal stream changes direction, is rarely at the same time as high or low water time. The tidal stream is usually weak at low water slack, building to its maximum at about half tide and gets weaker towards high water slack. Around some headlands the stream might run at up to 3-4 knots, so we don't do much Optimist racing near headlands!

Most Optimist sea sailing takes place in sheltered bays or areas of weaker tides, but even here there can be tidal streams of 1-2 knots. Even 1 knot has a significant effect on an Optimist. You can find out more about tidal streams from a number of sources.

- A chart, which will have tidal diamonds showing tidal streams, strength and direction before and after high water.
- An almanac which will have mini tidal stream atlases for all parts of the country. So before you go out racing on the sea remember, you need to know about the effect of the tidal streams, where and what time you will be sailing.

Tidal Effects

Wind with Tide

When the tidal stream is in the same direction as the wind, the waves tend to be smoothed out and much flatter than if there was no tidal stream at all.

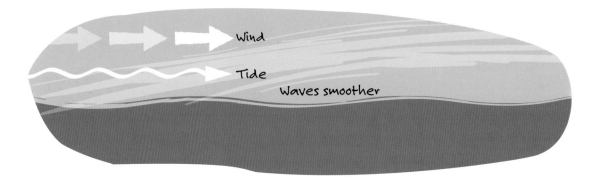

Wind against Tide

When the tidal stream is against the wind, it has the effect of steepening the waves and makes the sea state much choppier.

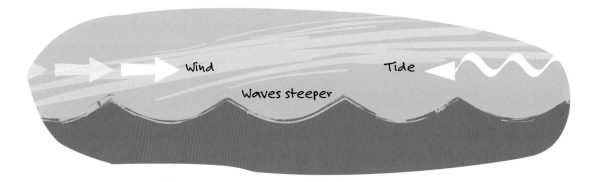

Wind across the Tide

When the tidal stream is across the wind, the sea state can become a bit confused.

Before you go afloat you should know what conditions to expect.

Sailing in a Bay

If you are sailing in a bay, you will find some interesting effects caused by the tidal stream. The direction of the main stream across the mouth of the bay will cause a huge eddy in the bay which will run in the opposite direction to the main stream outside.

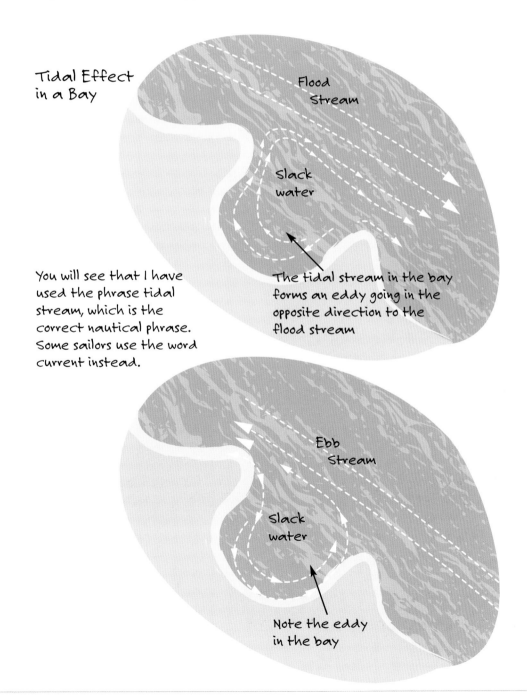

Tidal Effect in a Bay

Flood Stream

Slack water

The tidal stream in the bay forms an eddy going in the opposite direction to the flood stream

You will see that I have used the phrase tidal stream, which is the correct nautical phrase. Some sailors use the word current instead.

Ebb Stream

Slack water

Note the eddy in the bay

Sailing up an Estuary

In an estuary the tidal stream tends to rush in and rush back out again. The deeper water runs faster and the shallower water, affected by the friction of the sea bed, runs slower. If you are sailing against the tide you need to sail up the edges in shallow water and if you are sailing with the tide, sail in the deeper faster water. The following, illustrates an estuary.

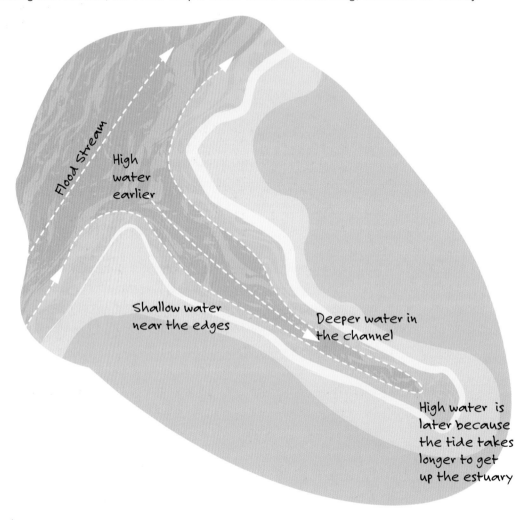

Flood Stream

High water earlier

Shallow water near the edges

Deeper water in the channel

High water is later because the tide takes longer to get up the estuary

Land

Shallow water tidal stream is weaker

Land

Deeper water tides run stronger

Tidal Effect on Starting

You should now be thinking - what effect might the tidal stream have on the start line? There are a lot of answers!

One nautical mile per hour is 1852 metres per hour, so 0 .1 of a nautical mile is 185 metres an hour. If the tidal stream is going just 0.1 knot against you, it equals 3 metres or one boat length in a minute. If the tidal stream is doing 0.5 knots against you, you will drift 15 metres or 5 boat lengths in a minute.

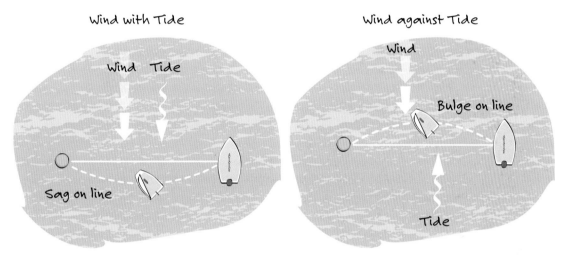

Now you can see how important the tidal stream really is.

Check Drift

If you want to check how strong the tidal stream is, sit next to the committee boat and hover. Check how far in which direction you drift in 30 seconds or a minute.

You can use a tide stick to estimate the strength of the tidal stream, which can be as simple as a weighted tube or plastic bottle. Drop it into the water next to an anchored boat or buoy and check the drift.

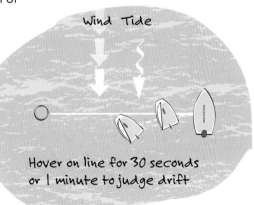

When wind and tide are together you will be pushed well back from the line, which often results in what we call line sag. If the stream is going upwind you will be at risk of being carried over the start line before start time, this often results in lots of general recalls.

Wind Across Tide

This is an interesting challenge for any Oppy sailor. You could be pushed either towards the pin end, or the committee boat. You need to avoid the end that the tide is going towards. In the illustration you will see that boat A is relatively lifted off the start and boat B is headed. Crossing the start line on starboard is easier.

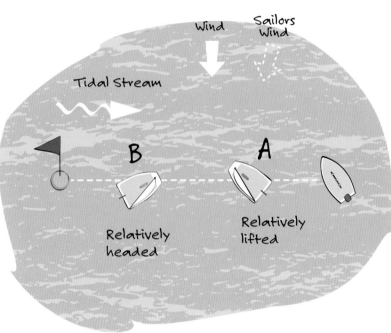

Tide across the course effect on starting

Tide Across the Course

If the tide is across the course going from left to right, you will be relatively lifted on starboard tack and headed on port tack.

If the tide is going right to left you will be lifted on port tack and headed on starboard tack end, out of trouble and in clean air.

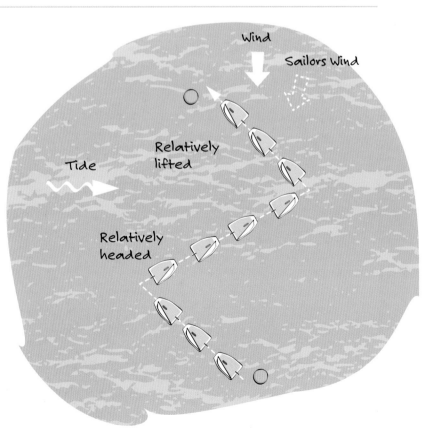

Lee Bow Effect

Sometimes when sailing on very tidal water – for example an estuary, or on a very one sided windward leg – you might find that if the tide is running across the course, you can use the tide to help to push your boat to windward by having the tide on your lee bow.

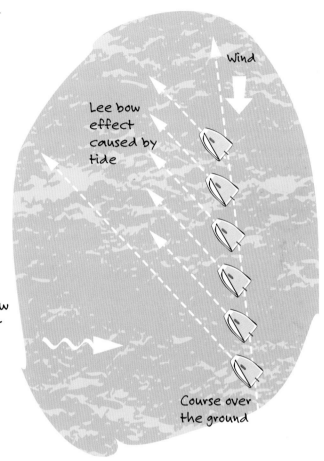

Wind

Lee bow effect caused by tide

The Lee Bow Effect

Course over the ground

The Sailor's Wind

The wind a sailor can feel is caused by the effect of the tidal stream. It is to the right of true wind, if the tidal stream is going from left to right, and right of the true wind if the tidal stream is going right to left.

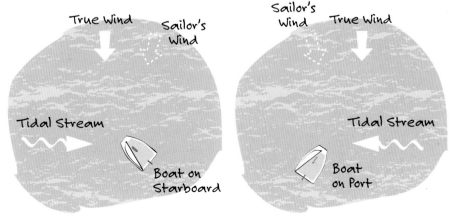

True Wind · Sailor's Wind

Tidal Stream

Boat on Starboard

Sailor's Wind · True Wind

Tidal Stream

Boat on Port

Tidal Effect on the Windward Mark

When the tidal steam is with the wind, it makes the laylines much higher and if you tack too early you will fail to make the mark – this often leads to pile ups.

If the tide is opposite the wind, it makes the laylines easier and there is often a gap at the windward mark as boats are pushed beyond the mark.

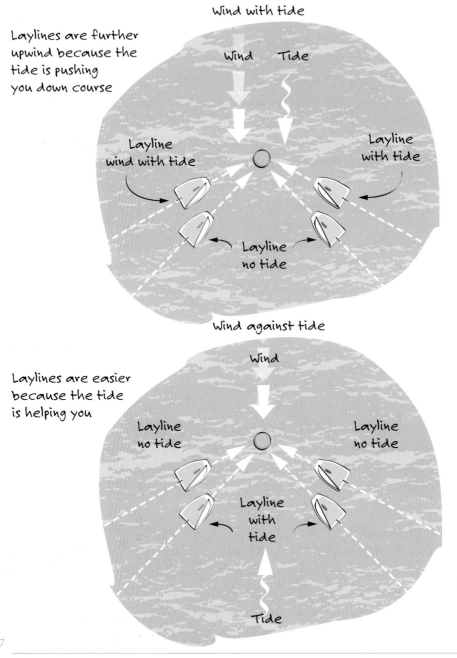

Wind with tide

Laylines are further upwind because the tide is pushing you down course

Wind   Tide

Layline wind with tide

Layline with tide

Layline no tide

Wind against tide

Laylines are easier because the tide is helping you

Wind

Layline no tide

Layline no tide

Layline with tide

Tide

Tidal Effect on a Reach

- If you are sailing on a reach in a tidal location, you can make big gains if you know what the tide is doing.
- When the wind is against tide, most of the fleet will be swept well upwind of the straight (rhumb) line towards the reaching mark.
- By sailing low you can make big gains.
- By using a transit between the reaching mark and the shore, check that you aren't being swept upwind.
- On a reach you need to get a transit through the reach mark to the shore, this will help you see if you are being taken high or low of the mark.
- If the wind is with the tide, you might have to sail higher to avoid being swept past the reach mark.
- When the wind is against the tide, avoid sailing very high to the mark otherwise you will have to run down to the mark against the tide, which is very slow.

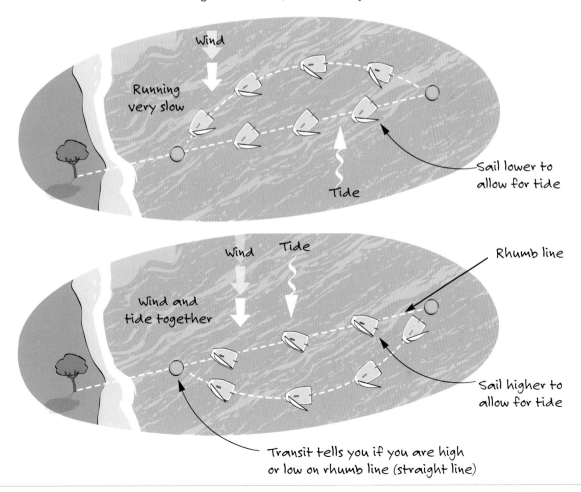

Tidal Effect on a Run

Tidal stream can have a significant effect on a run, particularly if the tide is running across the course. The illustration shows you this effect. Remember to always check where you are down the run by using a transit.

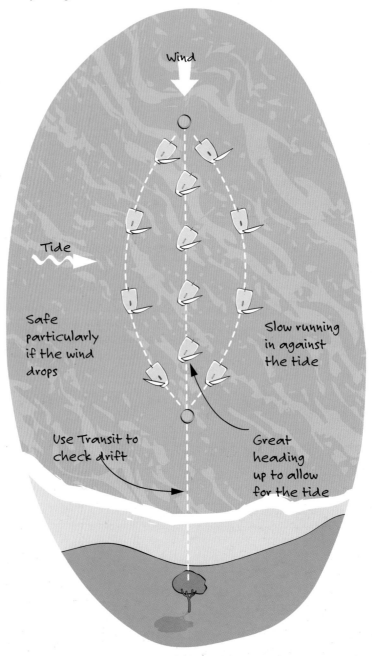

Wind

Tide

Safe particularly if the wind drops

Slow running in against the tide

Use Transit to check drift

Great heading up to allow for the tide

Sailing on a run with the tide across the course

EDDY BEHIND BUOY

4

TIDAL STREAM

Buoy leaning downtide. Tide is going from right to left.

Some sailors have a compass because it's a must have gadget. Everyone else has one so it must be able to make them sail faster. Other sailors spend ages looking at their compass and haven't a clue what is does. Let's take a look at the compass, how it works and how it can help you.

Why Use a Compass?

Good question! A compass is really useful to confirm what direction you are sailing and can confirm what you observe on the water. It can give you a reality check if you lose concentration and have one of those vacant moments. It will help you understand shifts and what the bias of the start line is. But be aware a compass can also be a massive distraction if you don't know how to use it!

Types of Compass

The most popular type fits on to the back side of your bow thwart and has a glass bowl facing you or on the top. Modern tactical compasses are segregated into 18 degree sections around the 360 degree circle giving 20 segments.

The compass has lubber lines so that you can read it at an angle, allowing you to read the compass while you are hiking. You need to be aware that in gusty conditions you will be able to point higher in the gusts and lower in the lulls even if the wind hasn't shifted. Remember those velocity shifts.

The clever thing about a tactical compass is that if you are reading 10 on one tack when you tack again you will be reading 0. If the number goes down on starboard tack you have been lifted and if it goes up on port tack you have also been lifted. Some sailors use a permanent pen to mark their thwarts with a plus or minus sign for a lift on each tack so they don't forget!

Compass mounted on bow thwart.

The only problem is that each segment is 18 degrees – that's a lot, so if you are sailing and you are headed by one segment it is a big header (18 degrees). Often a 10 degree shift or less would usually be worth tacking on.

Some sailors just use a normal compass with a 360 degree compass rose. These compasses work well, you just need to remember the heading on each tack.

Compass points to north.

Tactical scale in yellow.

When you are sailing upwind out to sea a compass can be really useful.

Compass Uses

There are a number of uses and as far as Oppy sailors are concerned the main ones are:

The windward mark	Point at the windward mark to get its bearing.
The wind direction	Point head to wind and get the wind bearing.
Confirming a wind shift	You think you are gradually being headed and your compass confirms it.
Working out the bias on the line	Work out the compass bearing of the line, then the wind, and knock 90 degrees off the wind bearing. If the difference is less than 90 degrees it is biased to the port end and more than 90 degrees it is biased to the starboard end.

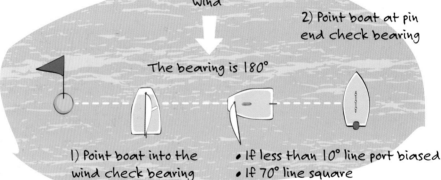

Wind

The bearing is 180°

2) Point boat at pin end check bearing

1) Point boat into the wind check bearing

- If less than 10° line port biased
- If 70° line square
- If more than 10° biased to starboard

Dealing with persistent shifts or oscillations	Your compass will confirm that you are being gradually headed or lifted which might not be so obvious to your eyes.
Entertainment Value	Compasses often provide some entertainment. It's a good idea to tie it in, otherwise when you capsize, it disappears and when you turn your boat over and you have forgotten your compass, you hear it smash onto the concrete or you simply can't find it.

Make sure you etch your name on it as compasses do get mixed up!

Coach and sailor discussing using a compass.

Develop your starting skills

Getting around the course

Weymouth - Championship Sailing venue

Section 4

'Don't forget that when you head out onto the water you need to have a game plan'

Ben Ainslie
3 times Olympic Gold Medallist

Starting
Strategy & Tactics
Championship Sailing

Never underestimate how important the start is. The decisions you make before you start and your confidence on the start line will often determine up to 90% of how well you will do in a race. So to start well you have to collect information and make decisions about that information. You will then have the techniques and skills to start where you want to start and have options for after the start. You need to have a plan, but you also need to be prepared to re-plan if things change.

Sounds easy doesn't it, take a look at some of the skills which will help you become a great starter.

In a 100 boat start

• 5 or so will get an exceptional start.

• 20 or so will get a great start in clear air.

• 20-40 will get a good start but will quickly have reduced options.

• 30-40 or so sailors won't get a good start and will start in dirty wind.

You want to be the boat that gets a start that takes you into the best position start after start.

In major events the start can be very crowded!

Very close!

Start line

Try to be on the start line going fast in clear air on the B of Bang. Sounds obvious but look at any Oppy start line to see how many sailors just aren't on the line.

Pre-Start Stuff

You are now trying to build up a picture of what to expect on the race course, it is really surprising how many sailors don't bother with this information, leaving their start to chance.

Pre-start information can be worked on at home. What will the wind direction and strength be? Will the breeze be onshore or offshore? Will it be a sea breeze day? Will it be a shifty day when tactics matter more or a steady wind day when speed will matter more? Are there features such as hills, headlands or valleys which could change the wind direction? And if you are sailing on the sea what about the tidal streams and what will be happening with the waves?

Race Day

Double check the information you have gathered:

On the way out to the race course get a feel of the race course, don't spend all that valuable time gossiping with your mates. When you get to the start line you need to check the following;

- Look at the committee boat, how big is it, how far out does the anchor warp go, will it get in the way?

- Is the committee boat moving around a lot or is it steady?

- Look at where the flags are.

- How long is the line and how long will it take to get along it?

- Is there any tide on the line and what's its effect?

- How are the waves affecting the line?

- Look down at the pin, is it a buoy or is it another committee boat and will the anchor warp be a problem?

- Check upwind to see where the windward mark is.

- Check the bias (see page 169).

- Get a transit (see page 170).

The mast on the committee boat with the orange flag is the start line.

Check the Bias

Most race officers will try to set a fair, square line to the wind, a line which gives everyone the opportunity to get a good start. In practice it is hard to achieve, so one end of the line is usually closer to the wind than the other. Remember, if it is a shifty day the bias on the line can be shifting right up to start time. To find out if one end of the line is favoured you need to check the bias, there are several ways to do this.

- Point the boat head to wind, on the line, and look to see which end is closer to the wind.

- Sail down the line on one tack and when you tack, if you have to sheet in to go along the line, the end if you are going towards is biased, and if you have to ease your sail the other end is biased.

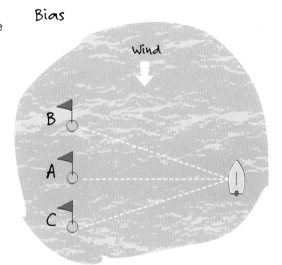

Bias

A Square line
B Pin biased line
C Committee boat biased line

- Use your compass – see page 162 if you need to check how to use it. There is a potential gain in starting close to the end which is closest to the wind - but not always. Why? Because the **biased** end isn't always the **favoured** end.

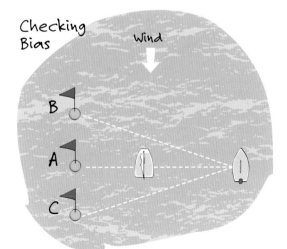

Checking Bias

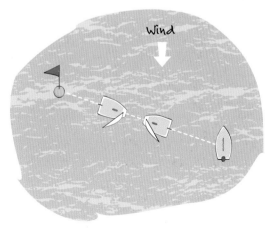

Point head to wind
Pin closer to wind - pin biased
Boat closer to wind - committee boat biased
Pin and boat level - square line

When you sail along the line, the end you have to sheet in more to get to is the biased end of the line.

Get a Transit

You need to know where the line is. One way is to line up the start boat and the pin with something on the shore, getting what we call a transit. This is the startline. Don't use sheep, people, or clouds as they tend to move. The problem with an on the line transit is that it puts you right on the line, so you need a safer transit slightly further behind the line.

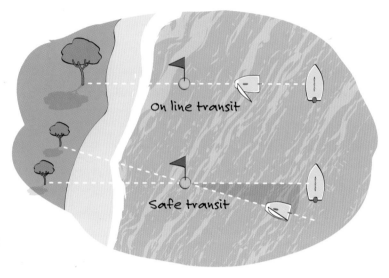

Over the Shoulder Transit

Many sailors don't realise that they can look over their shoulder back at the start boat and this can often give a much clearer transit.

You should always get a transit, but you won't always be able to use it because the line can become obscured towards start time.

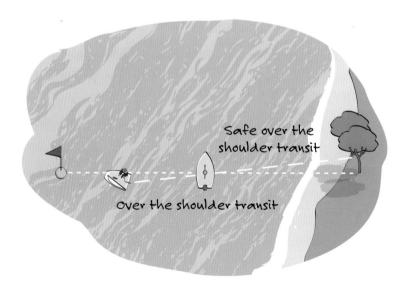

So if you lose your transit what should you do? Try to stay on the front row and don't allow the fleet to roll you. Go with them and try to keep your sail number obscured, trying not to be on the shoulders of a bulge or you will be easy to spot!

Line Sag or Line Bulge

When it gets choppy or there is wind with the tide, the fleet will be pushed back from the line. Top sailors will check this drift over a minute or so, to know how much they will drift. They have confidence to start early knowing that there will be loads of line sag. A good transit will also give you the confidence to sail out along the line while others are in the line sag.

Note sag in the line. A transit would be useful.

If the wind is against the tide on the line, the tide will tend to push you over and the fleet tends to bulge over the line. Wind against tide tends to result in lots of black flag starts.

When there is no distinct transit the fleet tends to drift over the line and then tries to get back behind the line. This causes a sort of creeping bulge. So watch out, and make sure you don't get caught by the Race Officer particularly if there is an I flag or general recalls.

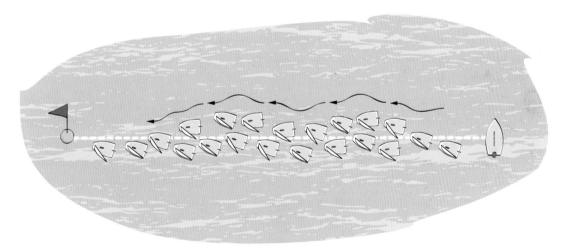

The creeping bulge moves down the line. It's easy to get caught over the line in a bulge!

So where do you start, biased end or favoured end?

The biased end isn't always the favoured end so beware of making big assumptions about where to start. An end might be favoured by the tide, the wind, a wind bend, a shift etc.

Turn over and we'll take a look at some of the options.

Pin Bias go Left

If the line is biased to the pin and you want to go left, start towards the pin. Exceptional starters might go for winning the pin but you have got to be really good to pull it off. Starting slightly further down from the pin jockeys can be a great option.

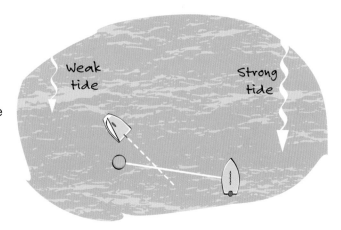

Pin Bias go Right

Basically forget the bias, the most important thing is to be able to tack off and go right straight away. So start towards the boat.

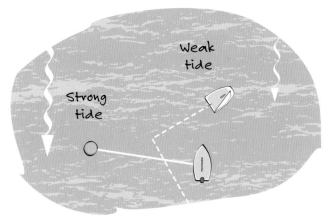

Boat Bias go Right

If the line is biased to the committee boat and you want to go right, start just down from the boat. Beware. There is likely to be a big mess by the committee boat.

The ability to tack off early is essential, to get into the wind caused by the headland.

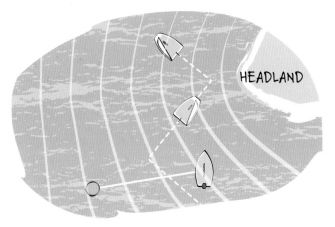

Boat Bias go Left

The important point here, is to start towards the pin holding your lane out to the left to get to the favoured side early.

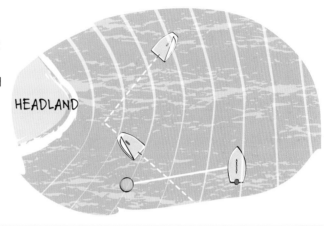

HEADLAND

Not Sure Which Way to Go?

If you are not sure what to do, you can start towards the middle and work up the middle until one side looks to be favoured or, just keep going up the middle using the shifts.

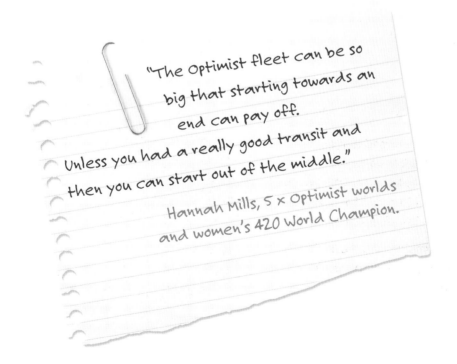

"The Optimist fleet can be so big that starting towards an end can pay off.

Unless you had a really good transit and then you can start out of the middle."

Hannah Mills, 5 x Optimist worlds and women's 420 World Champion.

Starting Skills

Slow Speed Boat Handling – The Hover

Your ability to handle your boat well while sailing very slowly is a key factor in getting a good start.

Hovering is a basic skill in an Optimist which needs a lot of practice. You need to be able to put your boat anywhere by using a squeeze of the mainsheet, a flick of the rudder, a heel of the boat, or altering your balance and anticipating what the wind is going to do next.

In particular you need to learn to hold a stopped hovering position anywhere between a close reach and head to wind. In other words you need to develop great automatic hovering skills.

A good way to learn is to practise sitting next to a buoy, until you can do it with your eyes shut in all conditions. Next, do it in pairs or threes and swap places. Most of the following skills are about slow boat handling so practise slow boat handling skills every time you go afloat.

2) You need to learn to hover for up to 2 minutes.

3) Hovering slowly towards the pin end.

4) Close quarters boat handling.

1) Hovering on the line next to the boat, it can be difficult to find a space.

5) Sailors putting their skills into practice on a busy start line.

Mind the Gap

Ideally you want to start with a gap to leeward and the bigger the gap the better. However if the gap is too big you are tempting other sailors to go into it spoiling your start.

To create a gap you need to squeeze up against the boat to windward, but not too much too early. Otherwise they will see what is going on and try to escape or, you will create a nice gap too early and someone will sneak in and fill it!

GBR tacks into a nice big gap made by SIN.

Sometimes sailors who create great gaps lose them by bearing away along the line and then heading up at start time. Often as they head up the boat slides a little sideways into the lee bow of a boat to leeward – a great race loser.

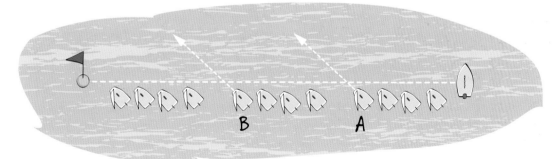

Boats A and B have created gaps to leeward to accelerate into. The boats in the bunches have no gap.

You need good boat handling skills on the line. Great sailors always seem to have more time to get themselves out of difficult situations, so let's take a look at some useful skills you can learn.

Dipping the Line

Provided that there are no penalty flags (I flag or black flag), you can be high on the line and drop down to just below the line at start time. You need to be well practised to really make this start work.

Win the Pin

This start isn't for the faint hearted. You either sail down the line towards the pin working out your speed, drift and time to the pin, then make a great start, or you are early and either bail out or try to hold the fleet up. If you are late you can bear away and sail fast towards the pin. Another alternative, is to hover outside the pin then sail towards the fleet coming towards you. If they are early you may need to sail along the line and find a gap and if they are late you can tack under the first boat, you're then in for a great start!

The Predator

We know that many Optimist sailors just rack up on the start line for a couple of minutes before the start. But if the wind is shifting around and you want to keep your options open, you can plan to come down the line behind the fleet on port tack and tack into a big gap that another sailor has just made for themselves. They probably won't even notice you and you can get a great start.

Lining up for a pin end start.

Sheet in and accelerate.

Cross the line at full speed.

A perfect pin end start.

Double Tack

A really useful technique, and you can double tack either slowly or quickly. You need to use a lot of rudder, mainsheet and boat heel to double tack in a confined space. But once you have learnt to do it you can tack into a gap to windward and tack back underneath the boat to windward creating a gap to leeward to power off into when you start.

Learning to tack close underneath another boat needs a lot of practice, because you need to think about where you want to end up. If it's windy and you aim for the middle of the boat you will probably end up with your bow too far ahead of the boat to windward. And if it's light wind and you do the same, your bow will be too far back. It is a matter of practising with another boat and getting a good feel for what works best in different conditions.

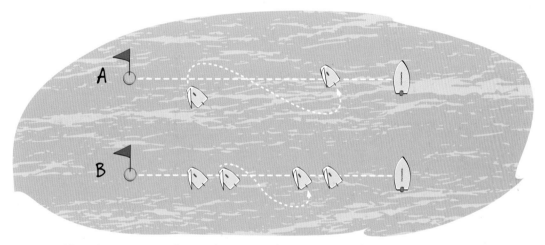

Start off with wide double tacks – then learn to double tack in a confined space

Drift

A simple skill often overlooked. Sometimes you will drift sideways and need to check the rate of drift over 30 seconds to give you an idea of just how fast you are drifting. You can also pull up your daggerboard to drift even quicker. To slow the drift push your daggerboard back down.

Sitting Back to Slow Down

Sitting at the back of the boat on the start line to slow down used to be quite popular but it's very easy to lose control of your boat. It can be useful sometimes just for a moment and then use one of the other techniques we have been looking at.

S Tack

This isn't really a tack it is more of a sail up to head to wind then bear away again which gains some ground to windward.

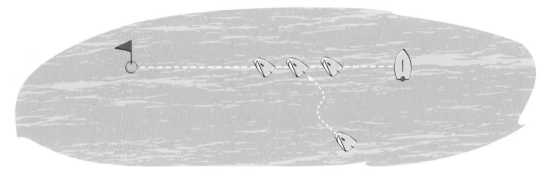

The 'S' tack is just a half tack

Very congested starts need good boat handling skills!

Stop Tack

Is a really useful technique which will enable you to tack your boat on the start line and position your boat accurately. Be careful because if you push the boom too hard the boat can spin around too much.

1) Sailing on a port tack mainsheet and tiller extension in back hand.

2) As the boat comes head to wind, push the boom out with your front hand to slow the boat.

3) Usually you let go of the boom and centre the rudder at the same time.

4) Step across boat - perfectly positioned.

Sailing Backwards

Sailing backwards can get you out of an awkward situation and is a very useful technique. So how do you do it?

• Point up to head to wind, then stand up and push the boom out stepping forward with your front foot over the thwart.

• To steer, as you push the boom out push the tiller towards where you were sitting and as the boat starts to sail backwards pull the tiller straight then steer.

• One great trick is to sail backwards out of the start line, gybe while sailing backwards, sheet in, sail forwards and tack again, ready to get back into the line.

Point the boat head to wind.

Stand up, step forward and push the boom out.

Bend your knees, and push the tiller to where you were sitting to get the boat moving backwards.

Steer downwind, smile, you're going backwards.

Acceleration

The ability to accelerate is an exceptionally important skill and takes lots of practice. First of all make sure you get the starting sound signals. What happens in the final minute is very important, a minute is a long time and you can do a lot with it.

Starting is all about speed, timing, distance to the line and dealing with other boats.

You can bail out of a bad situation with 30 seconds to go and still make a great start.

- Optimists often rack up head to wind but in order to accelerate you need to get your bow down to close hauled. You are then ready to get your boat moving fast.

- There is usually a power pause caused by having to sheet in the main. So just before you accelerate take up the slack in the main and you're ready to sheet in.

- Sheet in, but not too hard, because to start with you won't have too much flow over your foils. If you sheet in too hard too early you start to slide sideways.

- You can heel your boat to leeward and roll it flat in one smooth action to help you accelerate. If you do heel your boat to leeward keep your rudder straight as you roll the boat flat.

- Aim to be going as fast as possible and hit the line on the 'B' of Bang with your bow at least level with the boat to windward and try to create a gap leeward. See the acceleration photographs on page 216.

A holds the fleet up, then bears away

A

To accelerate off the start line you need to bear away to close hauled. Remember you can jab your rudder to windward to turn your boat to close hauled, but no lower.

More Acceleration

When you start do you think you should use the 'B' of Bang or your watch? It takes sound some time to travel down the line so if you are towards the pin and you are waiting for the sound signal, you might be up to a couple of seconds late to hearing it. Position yourself near the committee boat when you get the 5 minute signal and then trust your watch. Some sailors use big watches strapped to their boats, others count down the last 10 seconds in their heads. Some watches count down the last 10 seconds in bleeps.

Try to learn to count down the last 10 seconds in your head so that you aren't distracted by your watch.

Bigger sailors tend to take longer to build up maximum speed but slow down slower. Light sailors accelerate quicker but also slow down quicker.
You need to think about this when you are starting.

On a pin biased line you cross the line more slowly than on a committee boat biased line.

ANCHOR WARP

Start time at the pin, note the anchor warp.

What Happens If The Fleet Goes Early?

This is really tricky, most race officers will recall the fleet if there are a lot over the line, but this doesn't always happen. You can usually see if the fleet is shaping up to go off early.

If there is no penalty on the start, the fleet are usually recalled. If it's an I or black flag, sail numbers are taken and the numbers spotted are usually those seen easily from the committee boat or the pin. As the line becomes less distinct it is easy to get caught out. So if the fleet is going early it is good to have your sail numbers well covered!

Recovering from a Bad Start

Even with the best preparation it is still possible to end up getting a bad start. Someone can capsize on you or swamp you. You can get your hair stuck in someone else's boom or someone can come barging in spoiling your perfect start. So what do you do when it all goes wrong?

- Remember your plan. Is one side of the course favoured? Is there about to be a big shift? Often a sailor's first response is to tack off from a less than ideal situation to one which is far worse. You need to limit your losses and get going in the right direction in a lane as soon as possible. Sometimes you might have a bit of dirty wind but you are going the right way, in that case stick with it, until you can tack off and tack back again into a good lane. Remember always to think ahead.

- If you do get a bad start near the pin, either keep going or see if there is a route through on port tack. If there is, get onto port tack. If you are close to the starboard boats, transoms, you will get nicely lifted by their deflected wind. Then when one appears tack into a lane. If possible get into the windward side of a lane which will give you some space to leeward.

- If you start in the middle or towards the right, it's not too far to the right hand side of the fleet and you will find clear air.

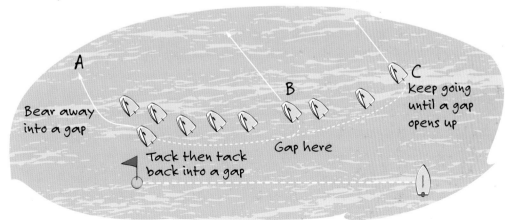

Starting Sequence

It is useful to make sure that you know the starting sequences which the race officer will use and the following details are a useful guide for you to use.

Class flag up	5 minutes	One sound signal
Preparatory up	4 minutes and any penalty	One sound signal
Preparatory down	1 minute	One sound signal
Class flag down	Start	One sound signal

The first race of the day should start at the scheduled time. After that race, race officers often leave the orange race committee flags down. Hoisting them informs the fleet that the next race will start soon.

There is a variety of preparatory flags

Blue Peter - no penalty.

I flag – If you are over the line in the minute before the start you have to round the ends. Not so bad if you are at an end, but if you are in the middle, it can be a long way to the end!

Z flag – If you are over in the minute before the start you get 20% of the fleet points added to your finishing score. If you are over at start time you are OCS [premature starter], unless you return and restart.

Individual Recall - On all of the above starts the race officer will sound a second signal and raise flag X (individual recall) if there is a small number of boats over the line at start time. If the individual recall is hoisted and you think you are over, you must return through the line. If it is an I flag return around the ends.

General Recall - If there are too many boats over the line the race officer will sound two sound signals after the start and raise the general recall flag (the first substitute). Racing will stop and everyone returns to the start line. After a short break the race officer sounds one sound and drops the general recall flag and one minute later goes into the next five minute sequence.

Black Flag - Most race officers start you on a Blue Peter or I Flag, but if the fleet keep going over, then the Black Flag appears. This means that if you are over the line within the minute before the start or at start time (and the race committee spot you) you will be disqualified from the race. If there is a general recall on a Black Flag, the race officer will usually put a list of the Black Flagged boat numbers on a board on the back of the committee boat. If your number is listed you cannot start that race and will have to wait for the next one. If you do start you will be scored DNE (discard non excludable) which means you are disqualified and you have to count the disqualification in your results. Occasionally on a Black Flag start, the race officer will display a board with black flaggers on it at the windward mark, if you see your number, leave the race course, smile and wait until the next race.

Postponement - Sometimes when the wind shifts before the start, the marks move, the committee boat moves, or there isn't enough wind. The race officer will often make two sound signals and raise the AP (Answering Pennant) which means that the racing is postponed. Be really careful when a Postponement Flag is up because, all the race officer has to do to go into the next starting sequence, is to make one sound signal to drop the AP then one minute later the five minute signal goes. This isn't much fun if you are half way up the windward leg practising!

O Flag
Warning

Blue Peter
Preparatory, No penalty

I Flag
Round the ends if over within 1 minute of the start or disqualified

Z Flag
20% Penalty

Black Flag
Disqualified if over within 1 minute of start

X Flag
Individual recall

First substitute
General recall

AP
Racing postponed

F Flag
To tell you racing will start soon

L Flag
Follow me

In this section we are going to look at strategy. The big picture of what's happening around the race course. We will then move on to boat on boat stuff – tactics.

The key components are:

- Keep it simple, if it's not simple it probably won't work.
- Work out your priorities.
- Get off the start line and have options.

- Sail as fast as you can maintaining a high average boat speed.
- Sail the fleet.
- Make tactical decisions when you meet another boat.

Before we take a look at each of these elements let's take a look at a simple diagram to help understand what's going on.

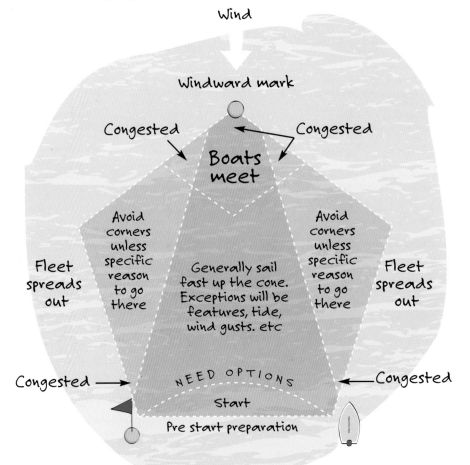

Wind

Windward mark

Congested

Congested

Boats meet

Avoid corners unless specific reason to go there

Fleet spreads out

Generally sail fast up the cone. Exceptions will be features, tide, wind gusts. etc

Avoid corners unless specific reason to go there

Fleet spreads out

Congested

Congested

NEED OPTIONS

Start

Pre start preparation

Start to windward mark strategy

STRATEGY & TACTICS

Work Out Your Priorities

Check out what the wind and tide is and will be doing. Are there any features which will affect the race course? Is it a shifty day or is it a boat speed day?

Get Off The Line And Hold Your Lane

You need to be able to hold your lane, so that you can carry out your strategy and not have your strategy dictated by others. Where possible sail on the lifted tack unless you have a good reason not to.

Options

If you have held your lane off the start and hold your lane for some time, you will have the option, to tack or carry on.

Sail As Fast As You Can Maintaining A High Average Boat Speed

If you have held your lane other boats are now starting to drop behind in dirty air and chopped up water. You will find that spaces are starting to open up, now you can apply your strategy.

Sail The Fleet

The ability to sail the fleet is essential: you need to be aware of where the fleet is at all times.

Tactical Decisions When You Meet Another Boat

These are boat on boat decisions. When you meet another boat when sailing upwind, you need to duck, tack or carry on.

Leverage or Separation

Let's take a brief look at leverage or separation, as it's sometimes called when sailing upwind.

Example 1:

When you get 100 boats on a start line of about 300 metres long, not long after the start the fleet might be spread out more than 600 metres. When the fleet is that far apart there can be big losses or gains, particularly if it's a shifty day.

Example 2:

If you are sailing against one or two other boats the closer you are to them the less the effect a windshift has.

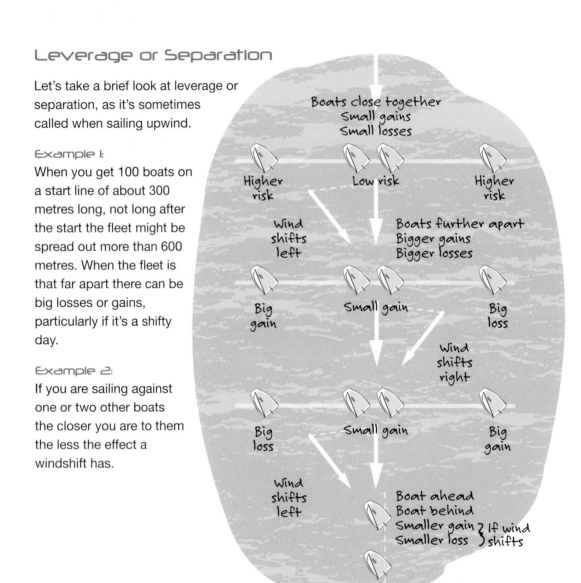

Boats close together
Small gains
Small losses

Higher risk   Low risk   Higher risk

Wind shifts left

Boats further apart
Bigger gains
Bigger losses

Big gain   Small gain   Big loss

Wind shifts right

Big loss   Small gain   Big gain

Wind shifts left

Boat ahead
Boat behind
Smaller gain ⎱ If wind
Smaller loss ⎰ shifts

Risk & Reward

So as we have seen, if you are close to the opposition you limit your gains and losses. If you choose to sail further apart you can increase the leverage and the risk. If you are covering a boat to the finish, you will probably want to stay reasonably close to it to minimise the risk. If you are not doing so well, you might choose to have more separation to possibly make a bigger gain or possible loss.

Sailing up the Middle

If there are no features which might result in you having to go left or right, then sailing up the middle of the course is the best option, tacking on the shifts and working a cone of about 60 degrees up the course. This is easy when you are leading but harder to do further down the fleet where you often get forced out wide left and right. Avoid the corners where possible when only a small shift against could leave you down the pan.

The 80-20 Rule

Sailing up the middle is great but if 80% of the fleet start to work to the left of the course and only 20% go right you need to be careful. Because unless you are certain that it pays to go right you are at great risk. The 80% will only need a small shift against you to be ahead of you and even if you are leading the 20%, you will be 81st and that's not much fun! So if the majority of the fleet go left you need to cover the left side.

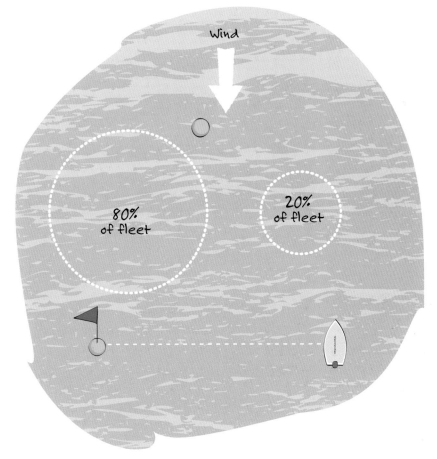

Generally stay with the 80%.

Positioning

Your positioning in relation to the fleet is really important sailing upwind. On a short windward leg it often pays to be on the right side of the course because you will be the right of way boat in traffic.

Sail the Long Tack First

On a one sided beat it's a good idea to sail the long tack first. If there is a further shift you can take advantage of it and it is easier to judge the short tack to the windward mark. If you are stuck in the pack, do a short tack to find clear air and a lane on port tack. Try to keep your options open and don't get to the layline to early.

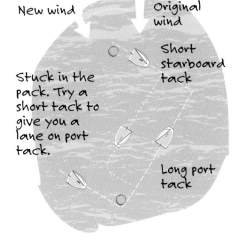

New wind   Original wind

Short starboard tack

Stuck in the pack. Try a short tack to give you a lane on port tack.

Long port tack

Lead to the next shift — if you can

Try to position yourself so that you can take advantage of the next shift first. If you are leading towards the next shift you can use it first and make a gain.

Don't sail to last — this is a classic problem for Optimist sailors

Sailors in the middle of the fleet often get lost and can't work out if they are on a lift or a header. If you find yourself in this position look at the tack the majority of the fleet around you are on, find a lane and get onto that tack. It will give you time to sort yourself out and get back into phase with the shifts.

One classic problem is that a boat to the left of the fleet tacks onto port and then ducks many starboard boats. Often the boats being ducked are on a lift and the more boats that are ducked the more places are lost. Eventually the sailor tacks back onto starboard and finds themselves at the back of the fleet. To make sure this doesn't happen to you, ensure you are on the same tack as the majority of other sailors.

When Boats Meet

Tack, Duck or Carry on

When boats meet while sailing upwind there are some important decisions to be made. The next section looks at the options.

You are the port tack boat

You need to spot the starboard boat early, this will give you time to make decisions (no crash tacks please). As the give way boat you have a number of options but the question you ask yourself first is, are you on a header or a lift? Once you know the correct answer you must now make some important decisions.

Do you tack early?

• Yes, if you are on the headed tack and tacking early leaves you in clear air.

Do you tack and lee bow the starboard boat?

• Yes, if you are on the headed tack and lee bowing the starboard boat would force it to tack off onto the header, leaving you on the lifted tack.

Tack to Lee bow

• A useful technique, which when used well is a great attacking skill.

Do you cross in front?

• Yes, if you are on the lifted tack and you want to get across towards the right.

Or do you need to duck?

• Yes, if you are on the lifted tack or if you need to get across to the right.

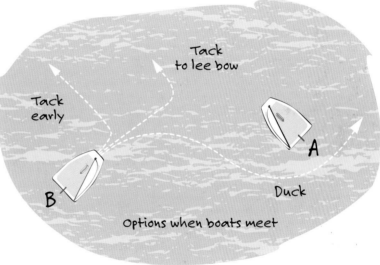

Options when boats meet

The aim is to judge your tack so that as you complete your tack you are positioned with your bow ahead of the boat to windward. The further ahead of the other boat's bow you are the better. You can gradually point higher and then the other boat will fall back into your dirty wind. If you misjudge your tack and the other boat starts to roll over you, provided you have space you can sail lower to prevent the opposition from rolling over you.

You are Starboard Tack Boat

If you are the starboard boat you have right of way and have your options too. Say you are on the lifted tack, have a good lane and are feeling happy. Then a boat on port tacks and lee bows you, well you wouldn't be happy anymore would you? So what could you have done to have prevented this? Well, for starters, always be aware of what is going on around you.

If a port boat may be able to tack and lee bow you, sail a little lower then when the port tacker tacks, point up and create a gap and carry on or, just be ready to point up as soon as the port boat lee bows you. Remember you can't just bear down on the port tack boat.

If the port tacker looks like they might just about cross ahead, tell them to carry on and let them cross. Then you can carry on, on the lift in your good lane.

> **Consolidate your Gain**
> If you have made a gain against other boats you won't have banked the gain until you have either crossed the opposition or rounded the windward mark.

Manage the Boat on Boat Stuff

As sailors get towards the top of the beat everyone converges onto the windward mark and many places are gained and lost by decisions made in the last quarter of the beat. It's just like snakes and ladders, so you need to be aware of what is going on.

• Are you on the lifted or headed tack?

• Are you sailing into a lot of traffic?

• Can you find a lane, and think several moves ahead?

• Can you find an exit route to get round the mark?

• Will the wind, waves or tide affect the laylines?

Laylines

- The key message here is to keep your options open. Try not to get to the laylines early, the later you come in the more you can use the shifts at the top of the beat.

- However if you are in the pack avoid getting onto the layline very late, or you might find it very difficult to find a space to tack and get round the windward mark.

Give yourself more room approaching the windward mark when it's windy.

Laylines tend to be easy to judge if you are at the front, but if you are further down the fleet laylines can be a challenge. There tend to be lanes of boats stacking up on the starboard layline, often many boat lengths to windward of the layline. This happens because boats are trying to find clear air. In this situation sailors coming in on port slightly down from the port layline who find a gap to tack into, can make big gains over those stacked up on starboard.

If you do find yourself on the starboard layline with boats tacking over you it can pay to tack early and find a clean air lane.

If approaching the windward mark on the layline and boats on port are crossing you, then tacking and giving you dirty wind, you might not be able to round the mark, so recognize this situation early and tack out while you can into a safer lane.

If you are sailing on the sea in waves, it can be difficult to judge the layline so come into it later and tack slightly above the layline or you might not make the mark.

The leading boats have an easy rounding, the boats further left are in lanes and there is a lot of dirty wind, GBR557 on port tack needs to find a gap and tack out starboard.

The Run

There are gains and losses to be made down the run so let's take a look at some of the possibilities.

- There tend to be fewer shifts to deal with downwind.
- Try to position yourself to take advantage of the gusts downwind.
- The leaders can usually pick a fairly straight course downwind in clear air, everyone else tends to spread out looking for clear air.
- If you are in the pack there can be a lot of congestion and dirty wind down the middle, so picking a side can be a real winner.

Rounding a Downwind Gate

Instead of a single leeward mark, in many bigger events a downwind gate is used to provide more options and to reduce the pressure on a single mark.

The gate marks should be about 7 boat lengths apart, but they do vary. So which mark should you round - here are some ideas.

- Try to plan ahead.
- If one mark is further upwind than the other you can make a gain rounding that mark but it can be difficult working out which mark is further upwind.
- When going down the run and there is a windshift to the right and most of the fleet are on starboard, tack, go round the right hand mark (looking downwind) which will leave you upwind of boats which rounded the left hand mark.
- If by going round one mark it will take you away from a strong adverse tide or into a wind bend, go round that mark.

- If it is a very congested mark rounding and one mark is very busy, it can pay to go round the other mark in clear air.
- Unless you are at the front of the fleet try not to have to tack back into the middle straight after a gate rounding. The water and air will be badly chopped up and you can lose a lot of places.
- Try to hold your speed and lane around the mark and then focus on your strategy and options.

Leading at the Leeward Mark

When you are leading by a good distance around a leeward mark you will want to defend your position, a good trick is to round the mark, go for several boat lengths and tack back. Then, when the next boat rounds the mark, tack, you will have good loose cover.

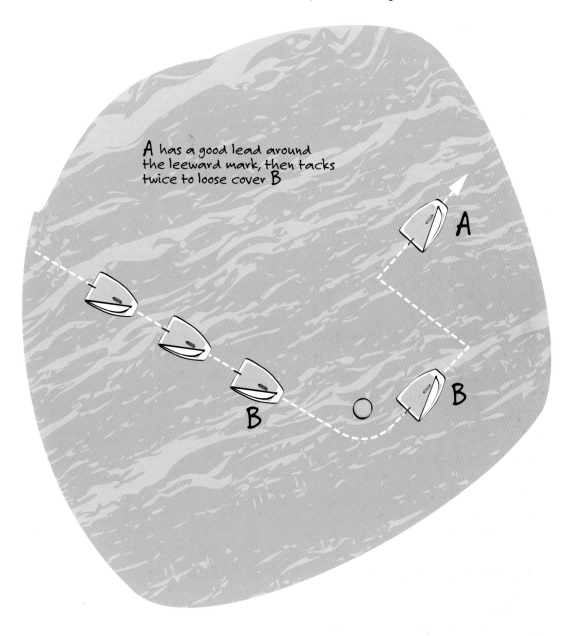

A has a good lead around the leeward mark, then tacks twice to loose cover B

This is a really important skill to learn!

Covering

You may find that you need to protect your position because you are near to the front or leading. In this case you will want to cover your opponents by keeping yourself between the finish and the opposition. If you apply tight cover, you will simply force the other boat to tack off, making you tack and cover again. A better option is to apply loose cover, then the other boat is more likely to stay on the same tack and when it tacks you hold on for a boat length longer and then tack. The advantage of this technique is that there is less likelihood of you making a mistake when you are tacking and it is much easier for you to control the other boat.

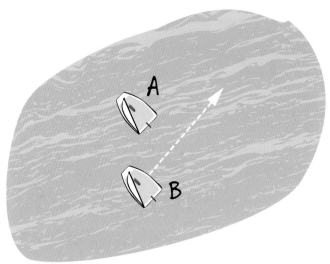

Close cover will force B to tack off.

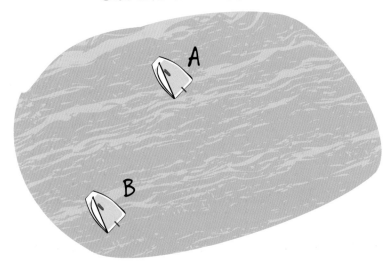

Loose cover will encourage B to stay on the same tack as you.

Finishing

There are generally two types of finish, either upwind or on a reach. Very rarely race officers may shorten the course and finish you on a run. The finish is generally a finishing committee boat with a blue flag and a pin mark or boat with a blue flag.

When you are finishing upwind there are a few things to think about.

1 Where is the finish? There has been at least one national championship where a sailor failed to go through the finish line because he didn't know where it was!

2 Which end of the line is biased? On many occasions boats sail along the finish line on starboard on a pin biased line, only to have port tackers ducking them and finishing ahead - not a good idea.

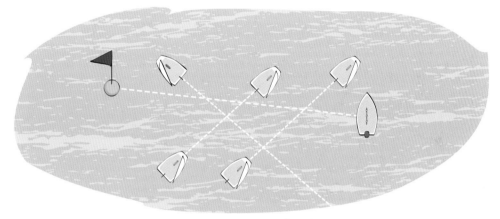

Finishing - watch out for a pin biased line, it takes longer to cross on starboard tack.

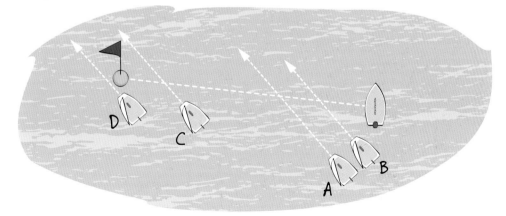

A has to give B room to finish. C doesn't have to give D room.

Finishing on a Reach

You need to sail as fast as you can. If attacking and going to windward of the boat ahead, be aware that they can luff you, or take you high then bear off to the finish. Rarely does it pay to go low unless the boats ahead get into a bun fight and go really high or if you are planing really fast.

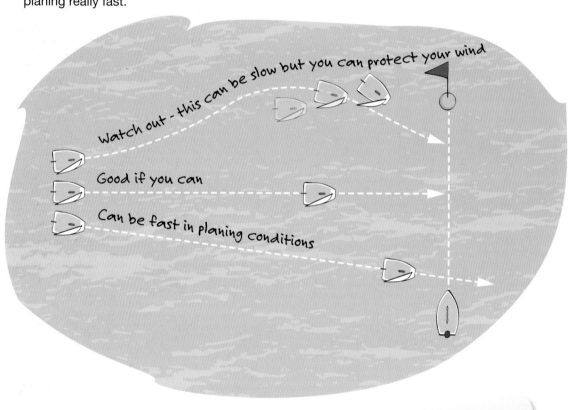

Watch out - this can be slow but you can protect your wind

Good if you can

Can be fast in planing conditions

When finishing make sure that your sail number is visible on the finishing line. If it isn't, write down the number of the boats which finish ahead and behind you in case your number is missed.

Very close finish in the Optimist Worlds.

Easier to cross this finish line on starboard.

Championships are fantastic events and you get to compete against other Oppy sailors you wouldn't normally sail against. If you go to international events you'll meet sailors from many other countries. Lucky enough to go to the Oppy Worlds, you will meet sailors from more than 50 other countries, an amazing experience.

A hotly contested start.

Championships are big events with lots going on, so you have to plan well and focus on the important things.

First find out where the event is. The class website or sailing club will usually give some information about the venue. You need to find out if there is a venue guide for the sailing area and what happens in different wind directions, also get the tidal streams information if the venue is coastal. You may need accommodation, so sort it out early. Get the notice of race, sailing instructions and entry form. Enter early – yes early, it stops stress and anxiety.

Representing your country is a great honour.

Boat Preparation

Make sure you have prepared your boat and have a good supply of spares. If your boat is going fast don't change anything before an event. If you have a new sail make sure you break it in before the event and get a good feel for it. Try out any new sailing kit before the event, so you are comfortable with it and know that it fits.

Some sailors are able to get to a big event a day or so early which means they can get settled in and out on the water to do some practising. That's great but not an option available to everyone.

Make sure you clean your boat.

Your Preparation

Make sure that you are alert, like a coiled spring and ready to race. If you have sailed too much in the run up to a major event and are tired and jaded, you simply won't perform to your potential. World Class athletes taper down the intensity of their training before a major competition. It's still good to do some venue specific training just before the event, but don't go out on the water for long sessions, 2-3 hours a day would be more than enough.

Don't be a Headless Chicken

In other words get down to the venue early. Some venues are huge with lots of space and some are really cramped. There are often queues of cars, parents, trailers and sailors so give yourself enough time to get organised. The first thing to do is sign on for the event. If it is a Nationals or bigger you will probably need to have your boat measurement checked.

Routines

If the event is over a number of days get into a daily routine and stick to it. Then you have no stress and can enjoy yourself.

Afloat

If it's an unfamiliar venue, make sure you get to grips with:

• The sailing area

• Features

• Wind

• Committee boat

• Racing marks

• Tide, if you are sea sailing.

• You have your food and drink for when you are afloat.

No Stress

Major events can create stress and anxiety. Stay cool – more on how to do that later. Parents should control their stress and anxiety, which can and often does spill over and affect the sailor.

Putting a Series Together

Consistency is the key to success, 10th one day and 110th the next won't get you into the chocolates. Richard Mason, 10th in the Optimist worlds in 2003 kept complaining that his results were really average and that he couldn't win a race, but he was so consistent that he finished 10th overall. He kept his eye on the big picture and he had one of the lowest overall scores of the competition.

Isn't it funny how sometimes you get out of bed with loads of negative thoughts and put in a really good days sailing?

One other point about putting a series together is that you could be leading a world championship for several days. Then in one race when things aren't going so well, you give up a little thinking that you won't have a race like that again, only to score a Black Flag and a sinking on the start in the last two races. You then have to carry the race you gave up in. This would be very tough, and the moral of the story is, **every point in every race counts.**

Chris Steel NZL 2007 World Champion with coach 'Wilizy'.

Gold medal.

Beacon Challenge Cup.

Rules when boats meet

Rules at marks

Rule 42

Section 5

'Its much more fun
when everyone
plays by the rules'

Chris Gowers
RYA Olympic Coach

Rules

Every sport has rules and for sailing the International Sailing Federation (ISAF), produce the Racing Rules of Sailing [RRS], which is revised every four years after the Olympic Games. The RRS are split into a number of sections. Most sailors mainly use two sections, the Part 1 Rules and the Part 2 Rules, occasionally browsing through the rest if they need to check on something. Although there are many pages to the rule book most Oppy sailors will be pleased to hear that there are only a small number of sections you really need to get to know in detail, so let's take a simplified wander through them.

Definitions

The first couple of pages deal with what we call definitions. In other words the meanings of the main words, so get familiar with them, it's not hard - only 2 pages.

Racing Charter

This is a framework for everyone involved in sailing whether a sailor, race officer, parent, coach or volunteer. It also covers on and off the water behaviour, including bad language, intimidation and bullying - all of which are unacceptable in our sport. You'll find the Charter in the front of the rule book so make sure you read it.

Don't Cheat

The basis of all of the rules is fair play with no cheating because our sport is mainly self policing. There are penalties for infringing rules, protest committees to hear protests not settled on the water, and a Jury to monitor on the water sailing at big events.

Part I Rules

These are the fundamental rules. There are only 5 of them but they are very important and include:

- Safety
- Fair sailing
- Accepting the rules

- Your decision to race
- Banned substances

Part 2 Rules When Boats Meet

There are more Part 2 Rules because Part 2 is all about what happens when two or more boats meet each other. There are only 13 Part 2 Rules and they are not difficult to remember. Here is a summary.

Rule 10 – Opposite Tacks

Port tack boat has to keep clear of a starboard tack boat, if you can't remember which is port and starboard, write it on your boom or thwart.

5494 on port tack has to keep clear of 5287 on starboard tack.

Rule 11 - Windward Boat

If two boats are overlapped the windward one has to keep clear.

4744 is the windward boat and has to keep clear of 5556.

Rule 12 - Same Tack Not Overlapped

The boat clear astern must keep clear of the boat clear ahead.

The boats clear astern have to keep clear.

208

Rule 13 - While Tacking

When tacking, once you have passed head to wind and until you are close hauled on the new tack you have to keep clear of other boats.

Or, if there are several boats tacking if you are on the left of another boat tacking, you have to keep clear, if you are astern you must again keep clear.

Rule 14 - Avoiding Contact

The rules say you need to avoid contact. But remember even if you are the right of way boat, you can be penalized if you didn't try to avoid a collision and major damage results.

5632 on port tack has collided with 5515.

Rule 15 - Acquiring a Right of Way

Even when you acquire a right of way you have to give the other boat room to keep clear.

A boat coming in from astern and to leeward on the starting line has to give the windward boat room to keep clear.

Rule 16 - Changing Course

When a right of way boat changes course, it has to give a boat on port tack room to keep clear.

Rule 17 - Proper Course

Proper course is the course you would sail in the absence of any other boats.

If a boat to leeward gets an overlap on a windward boat, the leeward boat cannot sail above her proper course to the next mark.

If you are a windward boat and there is another boat less than two boat lengths to leeward of you, you can't sail below your proper course, and if a boat astern is steering to leeward of you, you can't steer below your proper course, unless you are going to gybe.

Rule 18 - Marks

There are a number of rules which apply when rounding marks. Before we take a look at some of the more common situations, there are a couple of important points to consider.

3 hull lengths zone at a Mark

When a right of way boat which is clear ahead or has an inside overlap enters the 3 hull lengths zone it has the right to round the mark first.

Hailing

When approaching a mark a boat clear ahead or with an inside overlap enters the 3 hull lengths zone it can hail 'room' to make it clear that it has room to round the mark first. You might hear sailors hailing water or agua which are common in use.

3 hull lengths zone
around a mark

Start

At the start you can't ask for room on the committee boat, you can be squeezed out – so be careful.

ITA6983 needs to be careful.

Windward Mark

We can't have chaos around the windward mark so there are some rules to help you get round in an orderly fashion. So let's look at some situations, first imagine a 2 boat length circle around the windward mark, we'll call it the 2 Length Zone.

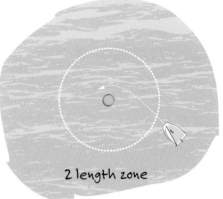

2 length zone

If you are approaching the windward mark on starboard tack and as you enter the zone you are clear ahead, you can round the mark. Any boat clear astern or to windward has to keep clear. A boat on port tack coming into the mark also has to keep clear.

If you have a boat to windward at the zone, you are entitled to room to round the mark and if you are to windward of another boat at the zone, you have to give them room.

Gybe Mark

Approaching a gybe mark with a boat overlapped outside you, you are required to gybe as soon as you can. If you are on your own you can gybe whenever you want to.

Tacking at the Mark

Coming into the windward mark on port and you tack under a starboard tack boat, outside of the zone is fine. But if you tack underneath inside the zone and the starboard tack boat has to sail above close hauled, it can protest you, so it's safer to come in on port outside the 3 hull lengths zone.

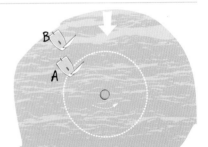

A enters the 3 hull lengths zone clear ahead of boat B and has room to round the mark.

Leeward Mark

Boats often sail at different speeds downwind, and we all know about the gains to be made by being the inside boat at a mark. So, if a boat clear ahead is inside the zone and you are flying down a wave outside the zone, you can't just barge in asking for room. This also applies to trying to go inside without an overlap at the zone when there are multiple boats inside the zone trying to round the mark.

If you enter the zone and there is a boat inside you, you need to give it room to round the mark.

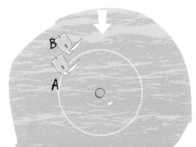

Boat A enters the 3 hull lengths zone it is overlapped by B & has to give B room to round the mark.

Not Happy - Then Protest

Protests are not about personal vendettas against another boat. You should only protest if you genuinely believe that another boat has infringed you and has not taken a penalty. If you are not happy with another boat and feel that it has broken the rules, protest them by hailing protest at the other boat and displaying your protest flag.

When you get ashore you usually have 60 minutes after the last boat ashore to register a protest. To do this fill in a protest form. Three people (the protest committee or jury) will hear the protest. They listen to your evidence and then the offending boat's evidence. A word of advice – be honest in a protest, because protest committees and juries are very good at finding out the truth. If there are any witnesses (which can be really helpful) they will be heard. Finally you will be sent away for a short while so that they can work out what happened.

When they have worked out the facts they decide if anyone infringed a rule. You and the other helm are then invited back into the jury room and then told the conclusion and if any boat infringed the rules. The jury can dismiss the protest, disqualify the other boat, disqualify you or even disqualify both of you!

Make sure you shake hands with everyone after a hearing and don't take the decision personally if it goes against you. Learn and put it behind you – remember no hard feelings.

Be warned – you might think you have a cast iron case but in reality probably only ever have 50% chance of winning.

Redress

You can seek redress in certain situations. If you finished correctly and the finish boat missed your number, fill in a scoring review form (from the race office) to get your score adjusted. It's good practice to always have a witness.

You can also request redress in other situations. For example, if a boat on port tack collided with you while you were racing, causing damage to your rudder.

Rule 42 - Propulsion

Rule 42 is interesting. A lot of thought has been put into this rule to make sure that sailors don't use illegal propulsion to make their boats go faster than anyone else.

The jury can whistle and yellow flag a sailor for a Rule 42 infringement. Sometimes they yellow flag you straight away, sometimes they see you infringing which puts you in a yellow light zone, and if they see you doing the same again they will yellow flag you. It is possible that the jury saw you infringing a rule from some distance away but take a while to come and flag you.

Usually the first penalty for a Rule 42 infringement is a 2 Turns Penalty. Penalties for Rule 42 infringements can vary at different events so check out the sailing instructions.

If you have been yellow flagged and you're not sure why, speak with the jury after the race and they will explain why you were penalised. The best advice is always to sail within the rules! Don't forget that you can also be protested by other boats for a Rule 42 infringement. From an Optimist point of view we will take a look at some of the key sections of Rule 42.

Rule 42.2a – Pumping resulting in flicking the leech

If you are sailing along and rocking your boat your leech is opening and closing – fanning you along very nicely! Be careful, all boats suffer from background movement particularity in waves, but on flat water there will be virtually no background movement so if your leech is opening and closing a lot and you are rocking your boat beware!

If sailing on a run and you have eased your sprit and your leech is gently opening and closing that's fine, it's not breaking Rule 42.

Rocking the boat results in flicking the leech, breaking Rule 42.2a.

Rule 42.3b - Tacking

You are not allowed to exit a tack any faster than you were sailing before you tacked. In medium to strong winds it is highly unlikely that this will happen, but in light winds it is possible, so be careful. **You cannot** do repeated tacks and gybes not related to changes in the wind strength and direction – Rule 42.2e. However, you are allowed to roll tack and use your body weight to make the boat head up or bear away.

The end of a good light wind roll tack.

Rule 42.3d - Starting

A common problem for Optimists is to become stuck head to wind on the start line. The Rules do allow you to jab your tiller to windward repeatedly to bear away to a close hauled course. As soon as your boat is on a close hauled course you have to stop jabbing your tiller.

Hovering on the line, you can jab the rudder until your boat is close hauled.

Start to sheet in.

Heel to leeward while sheeting in.

Accelerate swiftly away with a straight rudder.

Rule 42.2b – Rocking

Heeling your boat to leeward on the start line and doing one smooth sheet in rolling the boat flat is allowed. But be warned if you use a double action, rolling the boat flat and leaning in and rolling it flat again, this breaks the rule. If the jury is watching it would be an immediate yellow flag and a 2 turns penalty.

A Heel the boat to leeward

B Sheet in bringing the boat upright

C Sailing at full speed

Rule 42.2d – Sculling

Another action you can't do is to waggle your tiller backwards and forwards across the centre line of your boat, making your boat go forwards or stop you from going backwards. If the jury see you tiller waggling on the start line or anywhere else, expect a yellow flag as well as a pretty bad start. Good boat handling is much better than a yellow flag!

The circled boat is yellow flagged for sculling.

Rule 42.2a - Pumping

You are allowed to complete one pump per wave only to promote planing or surfing. This is permitted in Rule 42.3.c. One pump only not several small ones! If you pump to promote surfing and you don't surf and then try again, this puts you in the yellow light zone and if you do it again and the jury is watching expect a penalty.

When your boat slows down after surfing a wave and the apparent wind moves back, you are allowed to dump the main back out again. There are various names for this, the lasso pump or the negative leech flick are the common ones. You cannot immediately after the lasso; pump and pump again, because that would be repeated pumping.

Rule 42.2c - Ooching

Imagine that you are sitting on an office chair, the type with wheels on. If you thrust your shoulders back sharply and your bottom forward the chair will move sideways, that's ooching! If you pump to get surfing down a wave and lean back then slam your weight forwards and suddenly stop, that's ooching too! If the jury are watching you, expect a yellow flag.

Dynamically leaning back towards the back of the boat to get your boat through waves is perfectly legal.

The sailor has completed a single pump and leans back to stop the bow from burying in the wave ahead.

When the boat is surfing the sailor sits upright but you cannot slam your weight forwards, that is ooching.

Rule 42.2a - 42.2b - Bailing

You are allowed to bail, but you are not allowed to rock the boat. You can lean in to get a bailer full of water, it's best to do several quick bails and get rid of the water over the side of the boat.

You are not allowed to hold the bailer with water in it above your head - it's called shifting ballast and you will be penalised for doing it.

Rocking the boat repeatedly while you are bailing, the jury won't like and you should expect to get yellow flagged. Bigger sailors have no problem keeping their boats upright when bailing, but for smaller sailors it can be tricky because they have short legs, short arms and find it difficult to reach in, so smaller sailors need to practise bailing technique, so that it does not look like they are rocking the boat.

This sailor is bailing efficiently.

Rule 69

This rule covers gross misconduct and the penalties can be severe. Gross misconduct includes gross breach of a rule, good manners, sportsmanship, or bringing the sport into disrepute. If you hit a mark and the jury see you and you do nothing about it, you could be protested by the jury under Rule 2 fair sailing and also under Rule 69 – gross breach of a rule. The best thing to do is to avoid gross misconduct.

There are some additional rules that you need to have a knowledge of, these are contained in part 3 and part 4 of the Racing Rules of Sailing. Some of the more important rules you need to know are identified below.

Part 3 Rules

Rule 26 - starting races

This rule includes the visual signals (flags) and the timing sequence to start a race.

Rule 28 - sailing the course

This rules describes the course you must sail.

Rule 29 - recalls [Individual — General]

This rule covers what you must do if you are over the line at the start.

Rule 30 - starting penalties [Round an end and Black flag]

This rules describes the penalties which can apply if you are over the line at start time.

Rule 31 - touching a mark

This rules covers the rules which apply if you touch a mark while you are racing.

Rule 32 - shortening or abandoning after the start

This rule explains how a race may be shortened or abandoned after the race started.

Rule 33 - changing the next leg of the course

This rule explains how the race committee can change a leg of a course.

Part 4 Rules

Rule 44 - penalties for breaking rules of part 2

This rule explains the penalties for breaking any of the part 2 rules, including taking the 2 turns penalty.

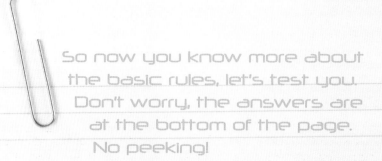

So now you know more about
the basic rules, let's test you.
Don't worry, the answers are
at the bottom of the page.
No peeking!

1   You are sailing upwind on a port tack and approaching a boat on
    starboard tack. Who has to keep clear, you or the other boat?

2   You are sailing on a reach and there is a boat to windward of you.
    Are you permitted to luff it to head up wind?

3   You are approaching the windward mark on a port tack within the two
    boat circle. You tack a boat on starboard tack who is approaching the
    windward mark and force them close hauled. Have you broken a rule?

4   You are about to round a leeward mark when the boat ahead of you enters
    the two boat length zone. You are clear astern. Does the boat ahead have
    room to round ahead of you or can you barge in?

5   You are approaching the finish, when a boat to leeward of you tries to luff
    you into the finishing boat. Can you ask for room to finish?

1. You do! 2. Yes you can. 3. Yes you have broken a rule - check which one!
4. The boat clear ahead has room to round ahead of you. 5. Yes, you can ask for room.

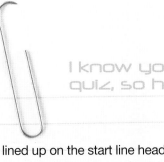

I know you really enjoyed the quiz, so here is another!

1 You are lined up on the start line head to wind, are you permitted to jab your rudder towards you to get your boat to bear away to close hauled?

2 You have just started a race and as you cross the start line your daggerboard catches on the anchor warp of the pin end start boat, but not the boat itself, have you broken a rule?

3 You are racing upwind on port tack and approaching a boat on starboard tack. Who has to keep clear, you or the boat on starboard tack?

4 You are sailing upwind on a windy day and you try to keep the boat flat by leaning out by using a series of body pumps, is that permitted?

5 You are approaching the windward mark on port tack within two boat lengths of the mark. You tack underneath a boat on starboard tack who is about to round the mark and force them above close hauled. Have you broken a rule?

6 You are sailing on a reach and another boat coming from clear astern tries to overtake you to windward. Are you permitted to luff the windward boat all the way up to head to wind if you want to?

7 You are bearing away around a mark from a reach to a run, and as you round the mark your boom hits the mark. Do you have to complete a 1 turn penalty as soon as possible before continuing racing?

8 You are sailing on a run in 15 knots of wind and a choppy sea state. How many pumps are you permitted to complete on each wave to promote surfing?

9 You are about to round the leeward mark. When the boat ahead of you enters the two boat length zone you are clear astern of it. Do you have to give the boat clear ahead room to round the mark or can you barge in?

10 You are approaching the finish on starboard tack. The boat to leeward of you tries to luff you into the finish boat, can you ask for room to finish?

1. Yes. 2. No. 3. You have to keep clear. 4. No. 5. Yes. 6. Yes. 7. Yes. 8. One pump. 9. You have to give room. 10. You can ask for room.

Mental Toughness

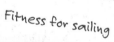

Fitness for sailing

Fuel for Sailing

Section 6

'To be the best you can be, you need to control the controllables'

Dr Ben Chell
RYA Psychologist

Goal Setting
Learning to Learn & Mental Toughness
Get Fit for sailing
Nutrition & Hydration

Setting yourself goals is a great way to make progress in your sailing. There are 3 main types of goals you will find useful.

1 Dream Goal

Your ultimate dream of what you would like to achieve. To start off your dream goal might seem unrealistic, sometimes Optimist sailors say their dream is to go to the Olympics. But that is an awful long way off, so it's a good idea to have some intermediate dream goals. Start off with to win a race or an open meeting, win a championship, get into a team or a national squad.

2 Outcome goals

These goals are about important performances where you need to perform to a certain standard in one or more events or races. For example to win a major event, get into a team or into a squad.

3 Process Goals

Finally there are process goals and these are the nuts and bolts which help you learn, make progress and achieve your dream goal. You use process goals to work out what we need to do in training sessions.

- To be a real winner you need to be fascinated by the process and leave no stone unturned in your quest for success.

- Process goals allow you to break down a technique into chunks so that you develop your skill.

- One way of breaking down the processes is by using 'SMART FUN' and here is an example.

GOAL SETTING

SMART FUN

Specific	Working on a specific technique like swapping hands when you tack not letting go of the tiller extension and making sure you rotate your shoulders forwards. Do this so that when you are under pressure in a race you will not worry about where the tiller extension or your body is. You can concentrate on sailing fast and the opposition.
Measurable	Out of 10 tacks how many times did you swap hands smoothly?
Attainable	With your current level of skill, is swapping hands 10/10 without letting go of the tiller extension attainable? Yes, it is realistic, but learn to do it automatically, eyes shut and without thinking about it.
Reviewable	Review or debrief what you have been working on, what went well and why and what are the lessons for next time. Write it down in your training diary.
Time phased	Practise the technique over a number of sessions on the water and maybe go back to a land drill to isolate the specific processes.
And Fun	The reason why you go Optimist sailing is to have fun, not to be miserable. But to have fun you need to practise. Remember, there needs to be a high fun factor in all of your training. It needs a purpose and it needs to develop your skill.

Performance Profiles

You can use a performance profile or spiders web to monitor your progress. The spiders web gives you a view of your sailing skills, mark yourself out of 10. It is really important to be honest when you score yourself. Everyone has something to learn and even the things you are good at need to be practised to keep them razor sharp.

The Spider's Web

Shade in your current level of ability, then see goals to improve, and decide to work on. The shaded areas are a sailor's current level. 1 = lots more work, 10 = perfect

Break down individual sailing skills into spider's webs too, so that you can be even more specific.

The Matrix Profiles

The matrix approach is to have a simple matrix of all of the sailing techniques on a computer. Use a simple traffic light system to score and monitor your progress and adjust the scores as you tick off can do elements.

● RED — Needs a lot of attention.

● AMBER — You have the basics but it breaks down under pressure.

● GREEN — Maintenance and tuning only.

Tacking	Flat Water	Choppy Water	Tidal	Improvement Goal
Light Wind	🟥	🟨		
Medium Wind	🟥	🟨		
Strong Wind	🟩	🟩		
Step Tack	🟨	🟨		
Hop Tack	🟨	🟨		
Strap to strap tack	🟩	🟩		

Gybing	Flat Water	Choppy Water	Tidal	Improvement Goal
Light Wind	🟥	🟨		
Medium Wind	🟥	🟨		
Strong Wind	🟨	🟩		

Mark Rounding	Flat Water	Choppy Water	Tidal	Improvement Goal
Light Wind	🟥	🟥		
Medium Wind	🟥	🟨		
Strong Wind	🟨	🟩		
Laylines	🟨	🟩		

We spend all of our lives learning new skills and everything we do is connected to our personality. Often we spend time learning new skills, but how often do we ever think about how to become a skilful learner? Interested? Then let's take a look at what it takes to become a skilful learner.

Ardvark

There are four main ways in which people learn new skills, These are:

Visual
Lots of people like to learn things visually, that's why we like demonstrations, pictures, diagrams, video, the PC and TV.

Auditory
This means learning by using listening skills and talking through what to do.

Reading
Some theory helps our practical understanding, many people like reading books.

Kinaesthetic
This is all about learning through doing. Getting out on the water and doing it.
The following well known saying can also help:

- I hear and I forget
- I see and I remember
- I do and I understand

And what about the ARD? Well it helps you remember the VARK! (Yes, I do know the animal is an AARDVARK.)

Imagery - the Mental Video

Just like you may look at a video clip of yourself sailing, you can also use your brain to make a mental video clip of sailing and situations you were in around the race course. It takes a while to develop imagery skills but it is very powerful and well worth it; imagery helps you internalise skills more quickly. You can use imagery to tack, start, round a mark or just to do slow boat handling.

RYA Skills Model

When you learn new techniques the RYA skill development model is really useful, and can help you make good progress. The four stages of the model follow and we have used tacking as an example.

Components
First of all you need to learn the fundamentals of the tack and develop simple routines.

Shaping
As soon as you have mastered the basics of a tack, the next stage is to learn to tack in different wind strengths and in flat and choppy water.

Diversion
In this stage your tack would be put under pressure. You could be for example, sailing upwind in a group in a simple race, considering other boats and where the next mark is and not thinking about how you are tacking.

Automatic
Your tacking will be completetly automatic when you don't have to think about it and can just get on with the race, for instance loose covering another boat in a race you are winning.

Small Digestible Chunks
When learning a new technique coaches will often use two main approaches. These are:

• **Whole-Part-Whole** – This is where you learn the parts of a technique and then join them together to develop your skill. For example, a tack can be broken down into components or processes which when added together will result in a skilful tack. This approach helps to accelerate the learning process.

• **Holistic** – Another approach is by watching someone else tack and then spend a lot of time learning how to perform the technique and become really skilful - this can take a long time.

Both methods have advantages.

• **Whole-part-whole** is often used for learning specific techniques.

• **Holistic** is often used to help develop tactical skills.

Memory

Memory is a funny thing, sometimes we can't remember something that happened five minutes ago but we can recall stuff from years ago. However, usually the more recently you have done something the easier it is to repeat it. As time passes if you don't practise your skill level will drop. That's why we always have to go back to the basics and practise them – the age old saying "Do simple things well" always works.

Sometimes the use of a keyword will jog your memory and phrases like:

• *Silky smooth* might make you tack super smoothly.

• *Rhythm* might get you sailing smoothly upwind.

• *Ease and squeeze* might get you using the mainsheet upwind.

• *Hooked* will get you thinking about the power in your sail.

You can think of your own favourite key words.

Mental Toughness

It doesn't matter which sport you compete in, you need to learn to deal with all the pressures which can occur in competition. Even the most skilful sailors won't win a race or championship unless they are mentally tough. So we'll take a look at some of the mental toughness skills you need to get you through a competition.

TCUP

When sailing in a race the most important point is, to make sure that you are thinking in the right zone at the right time. Sir Clive Woodward, coach to the World Cup winning England rugby team came up with the idea of TCUP (thinking correctly under pressure). He believes that if you control your mind under the most intense pressure then you control the game.

So it's really important to focus on the right zone at the right time.

On the way out to the start line, time to get your priorities right and control your emotions.

Confidence

You need to be confident both in your technical skills and decision making. If you doubt your ability it will affect your decision making undermining your confidence. The use of positive self talk can be really useful so instead of hearing yourself saying 'I can't', be positive and tell yourself 'I can'.

You need to be realistic about where you are at right now and be prepared to develop your skills. Even if you really can't do something well now, you need to be working towards 'I will be able to' and not 'I'll never be able to'.

It's easy to have your confidence dented and one solution is to put yourself inside a sort of confidence bubble making sure things that might affect your confidence just bounce off and go away.

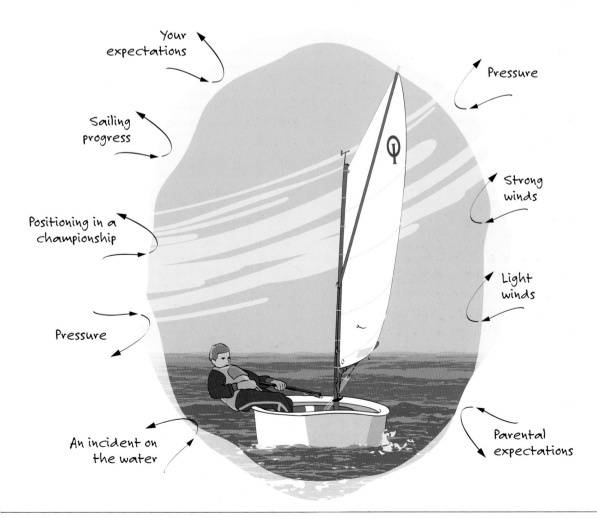

Confidence bubble makes pressures just bounce off

Your expectations

Pressure

Sailing progress

Strong winds

Positioning in a championship

Light winds

Pressure

An incident on the water

Parental expectations

Frustration

Have you ever been frustrated with your progress? Most people have and we know that it is very difficult to learn anything or perform well when you are frustrated. Causes of frustration include, not progressing as fast as you would like to, not understanding something, not doing as well as you would like in a race, parent's frustration that you are not achieving as much as they would like etc.

Frustration rears its ugly head in the following ways;

Blame the equipment
It can't possibly be your fault so blame the boat.

Blame someone else
Again, it wasn't your fault, it was someone else and you blame and shout at them.

Sulk
Yes, sulk, we all do it. You go off and won't talk to anyone, especially if you haven't done well in a race and your parents are on the shore waiting with your trolley!

Cure
If you start to get frustrated, take a break, talk to someone, or count to five and take a deep breath. Put whatever caused the frustration out of your mind and carry on – smiling!

It is important to have a plan.

234

Concentration

If you want to do well you have to be really focused. But with so much going on around you and so many other sailors to talk with, it's not that easy.

The zones model we looked at in the chapter on SPEED (page 91) will help you think about what you need to concentrate on and when. Remember the Me, Now, Next, Big Zones and of course, the Pizza Zone.

Worrying a bit - then take control?

Most people worry about things. It is natural to worry but it has its downside, if you are worrying you are probably not very focused on what you need to be doing.

There really isn't any point in worrying about the competition, the wind strength, the weather, your mum and dad arguing, someone else's new boat or the dead budgie. There's no point worrying about things you have no control over.

There's no point in worrying about things you can control, like your behaviour, your rig set up, or how you are sailing because you can control those things - so just get on with it and control them.

In other words CONTROL the CONTROLLABLES and don't worry about the asteroid charging towards the earth because you have no control over it.

Don't think about winning until after you have won.

Excuses

If you really, really want to make progress with your sailing, let there be no excuses, only possibilities.

Reflection

Reflecting back on what you have done in training or during a race, is a really good way to maximise your learning and it's good to write notes of what went well and why, also what didn't go well and what to do about it. The use of a training diary can be a really big help and here is an example.

Sailing Diary

Date: Venue: Event (training/competition):

Wind Speed   Weather Forecast

Wind Direction/Strength   Choppy/Flat

Rig Set Up   Boat Feel

Mast Rake

Outhaul   Personal Confidence

Luff Tension

Kicker

Sprit

Activities

Goal 1:

Goal 2:

Goal 3:

How well did you complete the **Activity**?

What did you **Improve**?

If you were being coached, what were the most important **Learning Points**?

What do you need to work on **Next**?

LEARNING TO LEARN & MENTAL TOUGHNESS

Expectations

Expectations can and do get in the way of successful performances in competition. They come from you, your parents, coaches and other sailors. What you need to do is to learn to manage these expectations. At your local club you may have an idea where you might come in a race and have targets to improve. If you are one of the top sailors in the country you might realistically expect to do well in a national championship because you know your level of skill in the competition. But when you go to an international event you have to focus on yourself and your sailing. After a few days of the event, patterns often start to emerge, you should then have a more realistic idea of what your goal should be.

Disappointments and Successes

Sailing is one of those sports where usually only one boat can win. Does this mean everyone else is a loser? No, of course they aren't. Everyone has different goals in a race so much so that there are often many race winners. If you are upset about your performance in a race, you need to quickly work out:

• What went well.

• What didn't work well.

• What you are going to do about it.

Then wrap the race up in a ball and chuck it in the bin, looking forward to the next race. Stop beating yourself up and be positive.

If you win a race, open meeting, championship or make it into a team, you should definitely celebrate your success. The better you get and the further you go the tougher it gets. The chances to celebrate real success become fewer and fewer, but don't go over the top because you are only as good as your last race!

Relationship with Parents

When you go to an event your parents will be feeling a bit of pressure as well, so don't give them a hard time. Be well organised, don't lose stuff and if your parents ask you to help or do something try to at least look interested. Don't play football or chat with your mates or spend time in the changing room while someone else rigs your boat. Try to be grateful, saying thanks helps heaps.

Coaching

Lots of sports have coaches to help accelerate the learning process. Coaches can be really good at helping you develop your skills. It can be good to work with a small number of coaches but beware if you work with too many you can get coach indigestion! All coaches are human and have their pet subjects and have slightly different views on things. That means **you** have to make **your** mind up what works for you. If a coach is working with you, they should discuss your needs with you and use a brief-do-review process to help you develop.

Coaching sailing is a practical subject, so if they have a high talk to action ratio, tell them actions speak louder than words! Video feedback of your sailing is a very useful coaching tool and a good way to help you learn. Remember a picture tells a thousand words.

Simple diagrams help the learning process.

Self Coaching

You cannot rely on a coach all the time and to do so is a bad idea as you need to learn to become independent. You should be able to go afloat with others and work on your skills. OK, it won't happen overnight but if you are an experienced 13 year old, you should be able to organise some of your own training.

Coaches should try to make learning fun.

Fitness is discussed a lot in Oppy circles and there is no doubt that fitness has its part to play in being an Oppy sailor. It is useful for all sailors to have a good level of basic aerobic fitness, flexibility and balance. Oppy sailors come in all shapes and sizes anywhere from 25-60 kg and as you grow bigger and sail in stronger winds you will need to develop more strength and the ability to hike for longer periods. Eventually you will want a more specific training programme.

Specific Stuff

As well as having good all round fitness, you need to have specific fitness for the following areas:

• Hiking for long periods.

• Sheeting in and out while you are hiking.

• Bailing.

• Concentrating while hiking hard.

• Big single pump above your head.

• Good balance and agility.

Activities

Apart from all of your school sports which are definitely good to participate in, there are some activities which are really good for sailing and they include:

Sailing

You just can't beat sailing itself, it's great for sailing fitness particularly the windy stuff, sailing upwind and downwind will really get your heart pumping.

Cycling

Cycling is great because it is so easy to do, great fun and it doesn't damage your joints because it is a non 'ballistic' activity, whether indoor or outdoor.

Cycling is an enjoyable way to improve stamina!

Rowing

Rowing machines are very popular and rowing is good for upper and lower body fitness. Make sure you are shown how to use the machine and either go for longer, easier distances to develop stamina or, shorter, harder distances to develop strength.

Rowing machine.

Swimming

A good activity particularly for the upper body, it's useful to develop your swimming technique making swimming all the more enjoyable.

Running

There's nothing wrong with running, but it's important to have good technique and suitable footwear to reduce pounding your joints and the risk of injury.

Weight Training

Optimist sailors won't need to do any weight training - just work on your aerobic fitness and agility.

Circuit Training

A really good activity which works all of your body and develops both aerobic fitness and strength. It's really good fun to do circuits with a group of friends.

Core Stability

It has been recognised that the upper body and lower body are linked by a variety of muscles. Often the stronger muscles do all of the work leaving other muscles underused and lazy. The use of the gym ball to improve and develop core stability has been used for some years and has become increasingly popular. The balls are readily available in sizes to match sailor weight and height, along with instruction manuals and DVDs. Perhaps the best option is to find a local class to join.

Developing core stability.

Remember when you are training;

- First you need to warm up with some easy aerobic activity to get the blood pumping around your body. Next you need to do some easy stretching. Regular stretching exercises will develop your flexibility. Remember no bouncing just progressive stretches.

There are lots of stretches and can include:

- Hamstring stretch.
- Bicep stretch.
- Tricep stretch.

- Upper back stretch.
- Crunch.
- Kneeling hip flexor stretch.

- Wall sit.

Using a rowing machine can help to develop your fitness.

Using a gym ball will help to develop your core stability & balance.

Indoor cycling is good for all round fitness.

Balancing exercises are good for sailors.

- Then you can do the meat of the activity, 30 minutes will probably be fine. You want to work at about 60-80% of your maximum heart rate which is about 220 minus your age. So if you are 12, your max heartbeat is about 208 and 60-80% of that is 124-166 beats per minute.

- At the end of the activity warm down and do some stretching to finish off with.

If you have several sports or gym sessions each week at school, one of the sessions above will be fine.

GET FIT FOR SAILING

Training Plan

There's not much point starting a training programme one week before an event. It's a good idea to keep a diary or log of your fitness sessions and the improvements you are making. The benefits are long term so if you are serious about your fitness you need to be doing 2-3 sessions a week, then just before major events, taper your training down.

Balance

You definitely need great balance to be a good sailor. Some sailors just seem to have natural balance and others really have to work on it. Exercises to develop your balance include:

• Sailing with your eyes shut. But don't sail into another boat!

• Transferring your weight from one leg to the other. Bend your knee, lower your centre of gravity, and you'll find it really easy.

• Standing on one foot (note the difference between standing on your heel or your toes). You need to get your weight onto your toes. Try practising with your eyes shut.

• Practise standing on a wobble board.

• Do lots of activities which involve shifting your balance both slowly and at speed, they all help your balance and agility.

Injury Prevention

As a young growing sailor you need to make sure that you don't injure yourself trying to keep fit or sailing your boat.

You can prevent injuries by using correct technique and not overdoing an activity. A lot of injuries are caused by carelessness in the gym, the changing room or in the dinghy park. All of which can easily be prevented.

Over-use injuries need to be avoided. There has been a lot written about growing youngsters and injuries. Good hiking technique as we have already seen can prevent a lot of lower leg injuries.

If you do suffer an injury that stops you sailing, make sure you get plenty of rest and ask for advice before you start sailing again.

Your body and brain take a lot of looking after and you need to make sure you eat the right food and drink to keep you going. Think about the activity you are doing and what sort of fuel you need to provide you with energy. It's healthy practice to get into good eating habits early.

General Food

There are a number of good books on the market which deal with athletes' diets, but if you have a wholesome balanced diet made of unprocessed ingredients you won't go far wrong.

Food for Sailing

Carbohydrates are really good, they release energy slowly providing you with a steady supply of energy throughout the day. If you need a quick fix there are fast release carbohydrates too. Many athletes who use a lot of energy such as marathon runners, bulk up on carbohydrates before a major competition, but really Optimist sailing isn't generally a highly physical sport, so a balanced diet is ideal.

• Carbohydrates include potatoes, pasta, cereal, baked beans, rice.

• Proteins, are essential for developing muscles and provide minerals that keep your body working properly, and are found in meat, fish, dairy products and nuts.

• Fats, some are good for you and are found in fish nuts and seeds. Others aren't so good for you, particularly hydrogenated fats, found in cakes and biscuits. Reducing the amount of chips and fried food you eat is sensible.

Breakfast

Breakfast is essential no matter how nervous you feel. Cereal, toast and fruit juice are really good. Avoid full cooked breakfasts, they take a long time to digest. Eating the middle out of a slice of bread does not count as a great breakfast!

As a special treat (if you win a hard race) cheesy chips are OK. But not too often!

Afloat

When afloat you need food which is going to provide you with a top up to your energy store and give you a quick fix if you are losing too much energy.

Consider the following:

Slow Fix
Bananas, malt loaf, pasta, jam sandwiches,

Quick Fix
Jelly babies/beans, jelly cakes, fig rolls, dried fruit, cereal or energy bars and carbo drinks.

What to Drink

The message here is drink little and often because even slight dehydration can affect your performance. You can do a test to check if you are dehydrated, simply check the colour of your urine which needs to be straw coloured or lighter. If it's darker then you are dehydrated. Generally an Optimist sailor needs about ½ litre of fluid for every hour afloat.

Specialist rehydration and carbo loading drinks are great, but don't use too much powder. Alternatively water with fresh orange juice and a bit of salt is easily absorbed and can be mixed to taste.

Post Race

If you have been afloat on a light wind and sunny day, you won't have used anywhere near as much energy as a cold windy strenuous day.

Match your post race food to what you have been doing. If it's been cold and windy when you get ashore, you need to build up your energy stores straight away. Pasta, malt loaf, jam sandwiches etc and fluid will start to replace energy used during the day. Make sure your dinner rebuilds your energy stores.

Parents take a keen interest
in sailing

Parent afloat supportng a sailor

Parents helping sailors launch their
boats

Section 7

'Always treat supporting your children as a choice not a sacrifice'

Peter Saxton
Parent

Parents & Sailors

This is the last section of the book and yet in many ways it's the most important. Without parents Optimist sailing simply wouldn't happen, so a big thank you for your enthusiasm, involvement and the time and effort you put into the sport and into sailing. I have met many, many fantastic Oppy parents who have a wealth of knowledge and experience and the following ideas come mainly from my experiences with them.

Small Beginnings

Parents are often as new to being a sports parent as some Optimist sailors. It takes quite a long time to learn all about sailing, and it will take time to become a skilful Oppy parent. Optimist sailing is just the first rung on the sailing ladder, early enjoyment in the sport followed by moving on into youth and senior classes will lead to lifelong involvement in the sport – so lots of stress and anxiety lead nowhere.

Stress

Like all good things, it's important not to overdo it and is essential that sailing should be part of a balanced life. Young children need home, school, friends, time for other sports, time to chill and of course time to sail. Parents also need time to do other things – parent time.

Sailing can lead to great emotional highs and lows which come from success and disappointment. It's important to keep a perspective, Optimist sailing isn't a life and death sport - even though it might feel like it at the time! Some parents want to achieve success vicariously through their children and will do anything for their children to succeed. If you are one of those parents you need to learn to chill out, it's OK to want your child to do well but don't over do it.

Doing Losing — How to Win

Losing is an everyday part of sailing, we all have to get used to losing; here's some key ideas to soothe away the pain and make a gain.

- Don't be afraid of losing, it does hurt but doesn't last as long as a headache.

- Learn to handle losing with dignity and compliment the opposition.

- You will be disappointed, but hey, you're still alive.

- My mantra – be excuseless. It's a winning strategy, but please don't come racing with me on a Wednesday night, I've at least 50 excuses lined up!

- Smile.

- Get on with improving, it's a lifelong occupation.

Shouting and Blaming

As much as we all are guilty of doing it, it doesn't work. It's not cool and is usually regretted afterwards… **don't shout and blame**.

The Optimist Family

Once you get into Optimist sailing there is a great social scene and a feeling of belonging. Don't keep your youngster in the class if they have outgrown the boat or are not enjoying themselves. Let them move onto the next class.

Many children get a great grounding in sailing through Oppy sailing and it's important to have appropriate competition. There is no point going to the nationals when the sailor is still struggling to get around a club race course. Some Oppy sailors don't win a lot of Oppy races but when they go onto the next class they can often do really well. It's all about individual sailor development.

Growing

Children grow and mature a lot during their Oppy years, from very young children who can only just see over the side, into unruly adolescents who challenge everything you say. As a sailor grows they have to change the way they sail the boat, and you need to have a lot of patience to help your sailor adapt.

Girls start growing and maturing between the ages of 12-14 and have often fully developed by 15-16. Boys on the other hand start their growth spurts later than girls between 14-16 and are usually fully grown by 18.

Maturity affects boys and girls. Boys have the classic mood swings and changes in behaviour, and with girls the development of menstrual cycles needs to be taken into consideration. During growth spurts, some sailors, even the best, lose coordination and need a lot of support to help them adapt.

You know that your child is growing because every so often you have to change their sailing kit and footwear. Some parents go for one size too big to make kit last a bit longer. But always ensure that a buoyancy aid is the correct size.

Be warned - parents often watch the sailing with binoculars!

Boys and Girls

Boys and girls are not the same and they can't be treated the same. And although there are no right and wrong answers here are some ideas.

- Boys usually mature physically later than girls and are usually stronger.
- Girls often mature intellectually earlier than boys.
- Girls are often more flexible than boys.
- Girls can often concentrate for longer than boys, who suddenly decide they want to go off and climb the drain pipe!
- Girls are often better at doing more than one thing at one time. It's called multi-tasking.
- Boys like to get on with it, girls often want more confirmation before doing something.
- Boys often respond to more aggressive language and girls more assertive, persuasive language.
- Girls can show more emotion than boys. Boys bottle things up more...
- Girls often want to talk about what they are doing and some boys just grunt!
- Often boys are very competitive and want to win (a throw back to the stone age when they would hunt woolly mammoths), and often girls need to learn about competing and winning.

The really good thing about all of these possible differences is that both girls and boys make great Optimist sailors and great competitors.

Independence Day

Over the years you will progress from parent to manager to taxi driver to financier to consultant, then you will become redundant. You will progress from being totally indispensable to being on the sailing parent scrapheap and you have to learn that if this happens you will have done a great job! It really is important for a young sailor to learn to make decisions - it's a life skill.

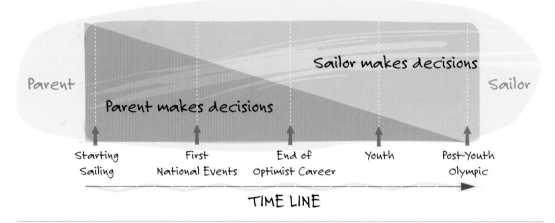

Expectations

We wouldn't be human if we didn't have expectations but we all need to recognise that even without us there, the sailor will feel some pressure. Putting more pressure on by placing further expectations on them, can be a major reason why a sailor doesn't achieve.

Telling your sailor that you'll buy them a new bike if they win, can place too much pressure on them.

Confrontation

Sailing events can be stressy affairs, you can usually tell the seasoned campaigners as they appear so cool, calm and collected. Whereas for the less experienced, everything is a rush. Get your priorities right and you will have plenty of time to sort everything out.

It's really important to avoid confrontation with your sailor during an event, power struggles usually end up in tears for all concerned. At least one sailor never made it to a world championship because of confrontation, and one probably because he didn't brush his teeth the night before the final day's racing at the selections! Try not to back yourself into a corner where you make a threat that you feel you have to carry out.

Sailor Space

Just before sailors go on the water they can start to feel a little nervous and need a quiet time to focus. When they come off the water, you need to be prepared with two responses. Firstly the sailor will be really happy and want to tell you all about their success, and secondly they just don't want to talk to you. Both are totally natural responses. Avoid saying how did you do, use power phrases like 'wow it was windy out there, must have been great fun' or 'hey that turned into a drifter' or 'want some food' or 'that looked really tough' or 'that was a fantastic gybe'. Avoid 'I was watching you all the way round and you missed that big shift' or 'that was a bad start', etc.

Coaching and Training Programmes

Most parents find it difficult to be mum or dad and coach, often it's a lot easier to get someone else to coach your children. Coaches can and do make a significant contribution to developing a sailor or a group of sailors.

- Coaches can do quick fix stuff like, introduce a technique and develop a sailor's skill.

- Coaches should be working on a brief-do-review coaching model.

- Coaches should also be developing soft skills like concentration, confidence, decision making skills, planning.

- Coaches can help with long term training programmes.

- Coaches should help sailors become independent not dependent.

- Parents spend a long time with sailors - coaches dip in and out.

- If you use too many coaches with too many different styles the sailors can get coach indigestion.

- A coach can do as much harm as good. So make sure the coach is qualified, and has a good reputation. Always discuss with the coach the aim of the coaching.

- The RYA provide very high quality national training programmes, a really good starting point for all coaching.

- Many sailing clubs provide excellent Optimist training programmes.

Things that Irritate Sailors

Try not to embarrass sailors in front of other sailors and don't nag them just before a race. Sailors can just about remember 3-5 things at most, so why not make it one or two things to be remembered and make sure that they are important positive things. Don't fiddle with a sailor's boat, generally the older the sailor the worse the fiddling effect is!

And finally...

Don't forget that you need to have the sailor's kit bag, with all belongings in your car at the end of the day. Check for yourself. Once I asked a sailor if she had put her bag in the car – 'yes' was the reply - and 4 hours later when we got home, no bag, it was still in the changing room. Always check yourself.

Thanks for being an 'Oppy Parent' - have loads of fun!

Sailing is a very competitive sport.

Remember, Oppy sailing can take you to some of the world's most inspiring locations.

Ben Ainslie - Finn Class, Olympic Gold Medal, Sydney 2000, Athens 2004 & Beijing 2008

Sarah Ayton, Sarah Webb & Pippa Wilson - Yngling Class, Olympic Gold medal, Beijing 2008

Ian Percy & Andrew 'Bart' Simpson - Star Class, Olympic Gold medal, Beijing 2008

'Many people don't succeed in the Optimist but succeed in later life so that's why I take a long term approach, I try to make sailing a sport for life'

Andrew Wills 'Willzy'
NZL Optimist Coach

Bailers	Used to bail water out of your boat.
Battens	Glass fibre sail stiffeners fitted into pockets on the leech.
Bear away	Turn the boat away from the wind.
Black flagged	Over the line and disqualified at start time
Block	Pulley for control lines to pass through.
Boom jaws	Plastic jaws which connect the boom to the mast.
Boom span	Cord on the boom which the mainsheet connects to.
Boom ties	Sail ties to tie the sail to the boom.
Bow	The front of the boat.
Bowline	A knot.
Bow thwart	The moulding which stiffens the bow area and holds the mast in place.
Buoyancy bag	Three bags in your boat to keep it afloat if you capsize.
Burgee	A wind indicator for the top of your mast.
Chine	The edge of your boat between the side and the bottom.
Clew	The lower rear corner of the sail.
Clew tie	Cord used to attach the clew to the boom.
Daggerboard	Like a lifting keel.
Daggerboard case	The case in which the daggerboard slides up and down.
Drag	Forces that try to slow the boat down.
Foils	Another name for daggerboard and rudder.
Foot of sail	The bottom of the sail.
Gudgeons	Rudder fittings.
Gunwale	Top edge of the hull – you sit on it.
Gybing	Changing direction sailing downwind.
Half hitch	Used to finish off a knot.
Head	The top edge of the sail.
Header	When the wind makes you sail lower than you where when sailing upwind.
Head up	Turn the boat towards the wind.
Heel	The sideways angle of the boat when sailing.

Hikers	Padded shorts for sailing.
Hiking	Sitting out to keep the boat flat.
Hover	Keeping the boat in one place- on the start line.
In Irons	Boat stuck head to wind.
Kicker	Known as the kicking strap – used to hold the boom down (see Vang).
Leech	The trailing edge of the sail.
Leeward	Downwind.
Leeway	The difference between the angle the boat is pointing and travelling when sailing upwind.
Lift	When the wind enables you to sail higher than you were when sailing upwind.
Line bias	The angle of the start line to the wind.
Lubber lines	Lines on a compass so it can be read at an angle.
Luff	The leading edge of the sail.
Luff tension	The tension of the luff.
Mainsheet	Rope for controlling the angle of the mainsail.
Mainsheet strop	A strop which reduces the amount of mainsheet needed and reduces windage.
Mast bands	The bands of the mast which the sail has to set between.
Mast clamp	A clamp fitted underneath the bow thwart to stop the mast falling out in a capsize.
Mast step	Adjustable fitting which controls mast rake.
Mast ties	Ties which attaché the sail to the mast.
Measurement certificate	The certificate which is required to race an Optimist.
Midship frame or thwart	The moulding which stiffens the middle of the boat hand and supports the daggerboard case.
OCS	Over the line at the start.
One turn penalty	One tack and one gybe
Outhaul	Rope which controls the fullness of the sails foot.
Paddle	Used to paddle a boat in no wind when not racing.
Peak	The top of the sail.

Pintle	A rudder fitting.
Planing	Going fast downwind.
Reaching	Sailing between sailing upwind and a run.
Reef knot	A knot for tying sail ties.
Rhumb line	Straight line between two points.
Rudder	Used to steer the boat.
Running	Sailing downwind.
Sail camber	The depth of the sail.
Sheeting	Pulling in or easing the mainsheet.
Snap shackle	Used to connect the mainsheet to the boom strop.
Spars	The mast, boom or sprit.
Sprit	Spar used to hold up the peak of the sail.
Sprit blocks	Used to tension the sprit.
Surfing	Picking up a wave downwind.
Tacking	Turning the boat through the wind when sailing upwind.
Tell tales	Wool or tape on the surface or leech of the sail which indicate wind flow.
Throat	The corner between the luff and the head of the sail.
Tiller	Used to steer the rudder.
Tiller extension	Attached to the end of the tiller.
Toe strap	Used when you are hiking to stop you falling out.
Tow line	Line for being towed.
Transit	A position or line produced by lining up two objects.
Transom	The rear of the boat.
Trim	The fore and aft balance of the boat.
Twists	The twists on the boom jaws controlling the luff tension.
Two turns penalty	For breaking part 2 rules.
Vang	Another name for kicking strap.
Wind indicator	Another name for the burgee.
Windward	Towards the wind.

Useful Web Addresses

Royal Yachting Association (RYA)	www.rya.org.uk
International Sailing Federation (ISAF)	www.sailing.org
International Optimist Class Dinghy Association (IODA)	www.optiworld.org
International Optimist Class (UK)	www.optimistsailing.org
International Optimist Class Associations	www.optiworld.org
UK Meteorological Office (weather)	www.metoffice.gov.uk
UK Hydrographic Office (see easy tides)	www.ukho.gov.uk

Sailing Diary

Date: Venue: Event (training/competition):

Wind Speed   Weather Forecast

Wind Direction/Strength   Choppy/Flat

Rig Set Up   Boat Feel

Mast Rake

Outhaul   Personal Confidence

Luff Tension

Kicker

Sprit

Activities

Goal 1:

Goal 2:

Goal 3:

How well did you complete the **Activity**?

What did you **Improve**?

If you were being coached, what where the most important **Learning Points?**

What do you need to work on **Next**?

The Spider's Web

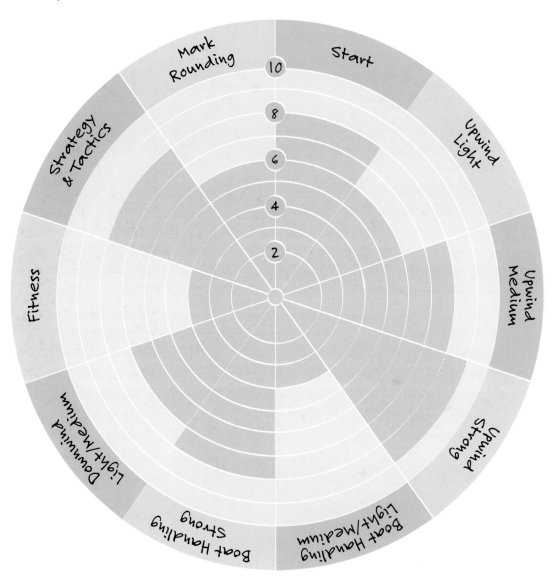

The Spider's Web

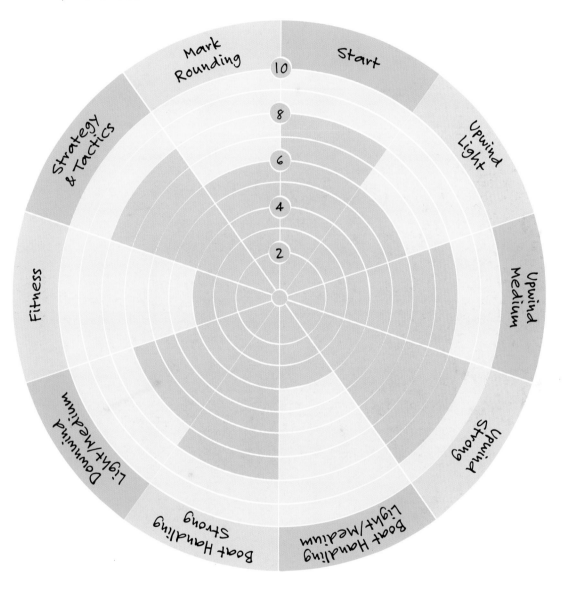